UNDERSTANDING
STOCKS

UNDERSTANDING STOCKS

Second Edition

Michael Sincere

New York   Chicago   San Francisco   Athens   London
Madrid   Mexico City   Milan   New Delhi
Singapore   Sydney   Toronto

12   LCR   21

| ISBN | 978-0-07-183033-1 |
| MHID | 0-07-183033-2 |

| e-ISBN | 978-0-07-183034-8 |
| e-MHID | 0-07-183034-0 |

This publication is designed to provide accurate and authoritative information in regard to the subject matter covered. It is sold with the understanding that neither the author nor the publisher is engaged in rendering legal, accounting, securities trading, or other professional services. If legal advice or other expert assistance is required, the services of a competent professional person should be sought.

> —*From a Declaration of Principles Jointly Adopted by a Committee of the American Bar Association and a Committee of Publishers and Associations*

Library of Congress Cataloging-in-Publication Data

Sincere, Michael.
   Understanding stocks / by Michael Sincere. — 2e [edition].
      pages cm
   Includes index.
   ISBN 978-0-07-183033-1 (alk. paper)
   ISBN 0-07-183033-2 (alk. paper)
   1. Stocks.   I. Title.
   HG4551.S564 2014
   332.63'22—dc23

                                                                2013033436

McGraw-Hill Education books are available at special quantity discounts to use as premiums and sales promotions or for use in corporate training programs. To contact a representative, please visit the Contact Us pages at www.mhprofessional.com.

To my mother, Lois, whom I will always remember for her compassion and generosity, and who asked for so little while accomplishing so much; and to my father, Charles, for his kindness and positive attitude.

To Anna Ridolfo, a close friend and loyal New Yorker, who devoted her life to helping others.

Contents

The Opening

A Much Improved Stock Book

Because of the success of the first edition of *Understanding Stocks*, my editor at McGraw-Hill asked me to write a second edition. I want to thank the thousands of readers who bought my first book and wrote to me with suggestions. Because of their ideas, this second edition is even better.

In this edition, I spent more time on how to make money using investing and trading strategies; how to find stocks to buy and sell; how to use market indicators to predict what the market might do; how to invest in alternative investments such as currencies, gold, bonds, and real estate; how to use exchange-traded funds (ETFs) and mutual funds to invest in the market; how to sell short; and how to use options to protect your stock portfolio.

In addition, I streamlined the sections on strategies and tools. Instead of simply listing every strategy and tool that is available to investors and traders, I introduced the most important ones. This will save you time.

I also created new chapters on how to minimize risk and avoid making mistakes. Finally, I included interviews with legendary investors William O'Neil and John Bogle.

My goal for this book is simple: I want to teach you what you need to know about the stock market so that you can make money when the market is going up and limit losses when the market is going down. There are no guarantees you'll make a profit, but at least you'll learn the tools and strategies before you invest real money into the market.

Who Should Read This Book?

If you are thinking of investing in the stock market or are already investing but losing money, this could be the most useful book you ever read. I grew up with the stock market, took the classes, read the books, talked to hundreds of pros, and invested and traded stocks. I also made every conceivable mistake, which I will help you to avoid. You could save thousands of dollars by learning from my errors.

As in my other books, I explain stocks as if you were sitting across from me at the kitchen table. My goal is to save you time and money while educating and entertaining you. In fact, if you are reading this book not to make money but for education or entertainment, my book should meet your needs.

This book will be different. It is designed to help you quickly learn how to invest in or trade stocks. Thousands of books have already been written about the stock market, many of them technical and tedious. I was amazed that so many boring books had been written about such a fascinating subject. Just like you, I hate reading books that put me to sleep by the second chapter. This is why I was so determined to write an easy-to-read and educational book about the market.

I wanted to write a book that I can hand to you and say, "Read everything in this book if you want to learn quickly about stocks." You don't have to be a dummy, idiot, or fool to understand the market. You also don't have to be a genius. After you read this book, you will realize that understanding stocks is not that hard. (The hard part is making money, but we get to that later.)

I also don't think you should have to wade through 300 pages to learn about the market. Too many books on stocks are as thick as college textbooks and not nearly as exciting. Even though this book is relatively short, it is packed with information about investing and trading.

No matter what your age or income, learning about the stock market is essential to your financial health. Even if someone else is managing your account, it's important you know how the market works.

The stock market is also the best place to make money. Fortunately, you don't have to have a fortune to make a fortune. On occasion, you might hit a home run and make a lot of money fast. For now, however, you have one goal: learn about the market. My goal is to teach you how to invest for a lifetime, not just for a few days.

You Need to Know the Truth

I wrote this book because I want you to know the truth. It upsets me that so many investors become victims of the stock market. The game that some people play is enticing individual investors into the market so that they can be talked out of their money.

Many insiders understand the rules and know how to use them to beat the market. In this book, I promise to tell you how the markets really operate. Without this knowledge, you hardly have a chance to win against the pros who do business on Wall Street.

Because the stock market is a brutal game that favors the house, you should know what you're up against before you invest your first dime. Unfortunately, you can't win unless you know how to play. One goal of this book is to educate you about the market so that you can decide for yourself whether you want to participate. By the end of the book, you'll know the players, the rules, and the vocabulary.

I don't want to scare you, just prepare you.

After my blunt introduction, you may decide that you don't want to have anything to do with the stock market. In my opinion, that would be a serious mistake. First of all, understanding the market can help you make financial decisions. The stock market is the core of our financial system, and understanding how it works will guide you for the rest of your life. In addition, the market often acts as a crystal ball, showing where the economy is headed.

This book is also ideal for people who still aren't sure whether to participate in the market or not. By the last chapter, you should have a better idea of whether investing directly in the stock market makes sense for you. Although I can't make any promises, it is also possible that understanding the market will help you build wealth. Perhaps you will put your money into the stock market, but I will give you many other investment ideas.

It's never been a better time to be an investor. Because of technology, you have tools and equipment available to you that your grandparents could only dream about. In this book, I will help you identify good buying opportunities and also develop the ability to determine when a stock or the market might be getting dangerous. It's not enough to know when to get into the market. You also need to know when to get out, and I help you learn to look for those signals.

How Much Money Can I Lose?

The first two questions that beginners often ask are: How much do I need to get started, and how much can I lose? Before I answer these questions, here is an e-mail I received from a reader: "I am 71 years old and am just starting to study stocks because I don't have a retirement fund to lean on. I am working three jobs and know I can't keep doing that for too much longer. What should I do?"

He wanted to know what strategies he should use to make fast money, including day trading or trading penny stocks. As you'll learn when you read this book, both strategies are extremely risky, especially for beginners. I feel badly for this man because he feels financially vulnerable. No one wants to wake up one day and realize that there is no money for emergencies, or even for survival. Therefore, one of the biggest mistakes is not investing at all.

Can you lose money in the market? Yes, you can. It is possible to lose part or nearly all your money in a worst-case scenario (such as a company going bankrupt). Although there are no guarantees you will make money, the stock market is still one of the best places to build wealth over the long term (and also occasionally make quick profits in the short term).

In addition, I introduce a number of strategies that will help you reduce risk. Although you can still lose money in the market, your goal is to limit losses so you can continue investing for a lifetime. My goal is to give you the strategies and tools to help make that happen.

What's So Great About Stocks?

Instead of working for your money, you can let your money work for you. You have a choice: You can keep money in a bank account, living paycheck to paycheck, or you can consider putting your money to work. Although the stock market isn't perfect, it is still one of the best ways to increase wealth over the long or short term.

At the very least, it's smart to learn everything you can about stocks. Do you think a particular stock is going to explode higher? There is a strategy for that. And if you are concerned that the market will go down and want to protect your investments, there is a strategy for that, too.

In my book, I am realistic. I know that most of the time, stocks are an excellent investment. But I also know that if you choose the wrong stock or the market crashes, you can lose money. So one of my goals is to help you protect your stocks and stock positions from large losses. You do not want to be a sitting duck, which is what happens when you don't take action when the market starts to fall.

Manage Your Own Portfolio

Another reason you are reading this book is to learn how to manage your own portfolio. Then you don't have to rely on anyone else to tell you how to invest in the market. Even if other people are managing your account, you'll have a better understanding of what they are doing (or should be doing). If anything, this book should give you the confidence to succeed on your own.

Don't forget this rule, however: No one cares more about your money than you do. If there is anything that stock scammers have taught us, it's that you can't trust anyone when it comes to your money. Learning about finances is the only way you'll know how to evaluate whether the people holding your money are acting in your best interests.

How the Book Is Organized

The book is divided into six parts. The first part, "What You Need to Know First," includes an introduction to the stock market. In Part 2, you will learn how to open a brokerage account and buy and sell stocks. In Part 3, you will learn investing and trading strategies including the strategies of legendary investors William J. O'Neil and John Bogle. You may be surprised that sometimes the simplest strategies are the most profitable.

Part 4 is the most challenging section. You are introduced to fundamental and technical analysis, which can help you determine which stocks to buy or sell. It's worth it to learn how to analyze stocks, even though it takes some time to learn. In Part 5, you will learn how to invest in other financial products besides stocks.

Finally, in Part 6, I show you how to become a successful investor or trader. In this section, you will learn why investors lose money, the lessons I have learned about the market, and my opinion about investing and trading. Finally, I list websites you can visit and other resources for additional help.

How to Contact Me

I congratulate you for taking the time to learn about the stock market. If this is the first book you read about stocks, I'm honored to teach you about this fascinating product. After you've read my book, other books about the market should make a lot more sense.

Thanks again for visiting. I tried hard to make this the most useful financial book you ever read. I wish you the best of luck, and I sincerely hope you find that learning about stocks is an enlightening experience, one that you will always remember.

Finally, if you have questions about my book or notice any errors, feel free to e-mail me at msincere@gmail.com or visit my website, www.michaelsincere.com. I always enjoy hearing from you.

PART ONE

WHAT YOU NEED TO KNOW FIRST

Welcome to the Stock Market

You may be surprised but the market is not that difficult to understand. By the time you finish reading Part One, you should have enough knowledge to sail through the rest of the book. The trick is to learn about the market in small steps, which is exactly how I present the information to you.

In my opinion, the market is relatively easy to understand (as long as you know the rules). The hard part is making money. Often, what prevents investors and traders from making and keeping profits is their own emotions, primarily fear, greed, and hope. One of the ways to reduce emotion is learning the facts, which is why you're reading this book.

Part One is important because it gives you a strong foundation before you start investing or trading. There is a lot of information in this section, so take your time reading it. I did my best to make it an entertaining read, but some of what you learn may seem confusing (at first). Once you make your first trade, however, it will be easier.

The Stock Market: A Huge Auction

Think of the stock market as a huge auction or swap meet (with some stocks, it is more like a flea market) where people buy and sell pieces of paper called stocks. On one side, you have the owners of corporations who are looking for a convenient way to raise money so that they can hire more employees, build more factories or offices, and upgrade their equipment. The way they raise money is by issuing shares of stock in their corporations in a public offering.

On the other side, you have people like you and me who buy and sell shares in these corporations. The place where we all meet, the buyers and sellers, is the stock market.

What Is a Share of Stock?

We're not talking about livestock! Actually, the word *stock* originally did come from the word *livestock*. Instead of trading cows and sheep, however, we trade pieces of paper (stock certificates) that represent ownership—shares—in a corporation. You may also hear people refer to stocks as *equities* or *securities*.

When you buy shares of stock in a corporation, you are commonly referred to as an *investor* or *shareholder*. When you own a share of stock, you are sharing in the success (or failure) of the business because you actually become a part owner of the corporation. As a shareholder, you get one vote per share at the company's annual shareholder meetings. The more shares you own, therefore, the more of the corporation you control (and the more money you could make if the stock goes up in price).

Most shareholders own a tiny sliver of the corporation with little control over how the corporation is run. That means you aren't allowed to boss around anyone in the corporation. You'd have to own millions of shares of stock to become a primary owner of a corporation whose stock is publicly traded.

In summary, a corporation initially issues shares of stock so that it can attract money. Investors buy stock in a corporation in order to participate in the success of the business. If the corporation does well, the stock price will probably increase, and you'll make money. If the corporation does poorly, the stock price will probably decline, and you'll lose money.

Stock Certificates: Fancy-Looking Pieces of Paper

Stock certificates are written proof that you have invested in the corporation. (Some people don't realize that you invest in companies, not stocks.) Although some people ask for the stock certificates so that they can keep them in a safe place, most people let a *brokerage firm* hold their stock certificates. It is a lot easier that way.

Note: A brokerage firm is a place where you open an account to buy and sell stocks. Today, most of the buying and selling is done online with an online brokerage firm. In Chapter 4, I show you how to open an account and begin trading.

To be technical, there are actually two kinds of stock, *common* and *preferred.* In this book, we are always talking about common stock, because this is the kind of stock that attracts the most attention from buyers and sellers.

Remember, not all companies issue stock. A company has to be a *corporation,* which is a legally defined term. Most of the large companies you have heard of are corporations, and, yes, their stocks are all traded in the stock market. I'm talking about corporations like Microsoft, IBM, Disney, Apple, Google, Nike, General Electric, and McDonald's, to name a few. Some remain privately held and do not sell shares to the public.

You Buy Stocks for One Main Reason: To Make Money

The stock market is all about making money. Quite simply, if you buy stock in a corporation that is doing well and consistently growing its profits, then the stock you own should go up in price. (By the way, the profits you make from a stock are called *capital gains,* which is the difference between your buy and sell prices. If you lose money, it is called a *capital loss.*)

You make money in the stock market by buying a stock at one price and selling it at a higher price. It's that simple. There is no guarantee, of course, that you'll make money. Even the stocks of good corporations can go down sometimes. If you buy stocks in corporations that do well, you should be rewarded with a higher stock price. It doesn't always work out that way because other factors are in play, but this is the risk you take when you participate in the market.

New York: Where Stock Investing Became Popular

Before there was a place called the stock market, buyers and sellers had to meet in the street. Sometime around 1790, they met every weekday under a buttonwood tree in New York City. It just happened that the name of the street where all this took place was Wall Street. (For history buffs, the buttonwood tree was at 68 Wall Street.)

A lot of people heard about what was happening on Wall Street and wanted a piece of the action. On some days, as many as 100 shares of stock were exchanged! (In today's market, billions of shares of stock are exchanged every day.)

It got so crowded in the early days that 24 brokers and merchants who controlled the trading activities decided to organize what they were doing. For a fixed *commission,* they agreed to buy and sell shares of stock in corporations to the public. They gave themselves 25 cents for each share of stock they traded (today we would call these people stockbrokers). The Buttonwood Agreement, as it was called, was signed in 1792. This was the humble beginning of the New York Stock Exchange (NYSE).

It wasn't long before the brokers and merchants moved their offices to a Wall Street coffee shop. Eventually, they moved indoors permanently to the New York Stock Exchange Building on Wall Street. Keep in mind that a stock exchange is simply a place where people go to buy and sell stocks. It provides an organized marketplace for stocks, just as a supermarket provides a marketplace for food.

Even after 200 years, the name *Wall Street* is a symbol for the U.S. stock exchanges and the financial institutions that do business with them, no matter what their physical location. If you go to New York, you'll see that Wall Street is just a narrow street in the financial district of Lower Manhattan. Therefore, the stock market, or Wall Street, is really a convenient way of talking about anyone or anything connected with our financial markets.

Two Major Stock Exchanges

After the New York Stock Exchange was formed, brokers trading stocks that didn't meet the requirements for the New York Stock Exchange traded on the street curb, which is why they were called curbside brokers. In 1911, these brokers became known as the New York Curb Market. In 1921, they finally moved indoors to a building on Greenwich Street and changed their name to the New York Curb Exchange. In 1953, the exchange was renamed the American Stock Exchange.

The third stock exchange was the National Association of Securities Dealers Automated Quotation System (Nasdaq), which was created in 1971. This was the first electronic stock exchange and members were linked together by a network of computers. (Yes, they did have computers back then.)

At one time, major U.S. cities had stock exchanges, including the Philadelphia Stock Exchange (which was our country's oldest organized stock exchange) and the Boston Stock Exchange, to name a couple. In order to compete more effectively, many of the smaller stock exchanges (including the American Stock Exchange) merged with the NYSE.

With the mergers, the NYSE became known as the NYSE Euronext. The Nasdaq also gobbled up some of the smaller exchanges but kept its name. It is guaranteed that in the future there will be other mergers and name changes.

There are stock exchanges in nearly every country in the world, although the U.S. market is the largest. Other countries with stock exchanges include England, Germany, Switzerland, France, the Netherlands, Russia, Japan, China, Sweden, Italy, Brazil, Mexico, Canada, and Australia.

Bottom line: All of this is interesting, but it doesn't really affect you as an investor. In the end, it doesn't really matter from which exchange you buy stocks, although more than likely it will be from one of the two major U.S. stock exchanges: the NYSE or Nasdaq.

Joining a Stock Exchange

It's not easy for a corporation to be listed on a stock exchange because each exchange has many rules and regulations. It can take years for a new corporation to meet all the requirements and have its stock listed for trading on the exchange.

For example, the companies that are listed on the NYSE are some of the best-known and biggest corporations in the United States—*blue chip* corporations like Walmart, Home Depot, IBM, Procter & Gamble, Johnson & Johnson, and Coca-Cola.

The Nasdaq, on the other hand, contains many technology corporations like Google, Facebook, and Apple. In addition, stocks that are traded "over the counter" (OTC) are located on the Nasdaq. By the way, there are over 15,000 publicly traded companies, with 5,000 stocks traded on the two major U.S. stock exchanges and another 10,000 smaller companies traded over the counter.

Remember, by getting listed on a stock exchange, its shares become widely held. When a company has many shareholders, it automatically gains loyal customers. Of course, by selling shares of a company-owned stock, the corporation raises money. That is the main motivation for a company to initially sell shares of stock.

Corporations: Convincing People to Buy Their Stock

Once a corporation goes public and allows its stock to be traded, the trick is to convince investors that the corporation is a worthy investment. Corporations do everything in their power to sell products, and also to attract money from investors. Bigger corporations spread the word through print, television, online, and mobile media. Smaller corporations rely more heavily on online advertising, especially social and mobile media, and also word of mouth, e-mails, and news releases.

Professionals connected to Wall Street always say good things about the market: They want the market to go up. If you're lucky, you'll also make a few bucks if you invest in a profitable corporation.

Note: After a company raises money by getting listed and selling its shares (via an IPO, or *initial public offering*) on the stock exchange, the company is uninvolved in trading the shares. All trading profits or losses made from the buying and selling of the stock go to investors, not the company. In other words, even if the stock price of IBM went up by 20 percent, the company gains only from the shares it already owns. It does not participate in the shares sold to the public. Nevertheless, companies like to see rising stock prices because it is good publicity. It also keeps the employees (who tend to own shares) happy. So companies want people to buy their stock.

On the other hand, if a stock gets slammed, this creates negative headlines, which companies prefer to avoid. So companies do whatever they can afford to convince investors (and noninvestors) to buy their product, which will, in turn, generate profits that motivate major institutional investors (pension funds and banks, for example) to buy their stock.

Now that you have some idea of what happens behind the scenes at the exchanges, I'll take you upstairs. First, I introduce you to the three types of people who participate in the market: individual investors, short-term traders, and professionals. By the time you finish Part One, you should have a better idea of how you can participate.

Individual Investors

Investors buy stocks in corporations whose share price they believe to be undervalued. They plan to hold those stocks for the long term (usually for years). Investors generally choose to ignore the short-term day-to-day price fluctuations of the market. If all goes according to plan, they find that the value of their investment has increased over time.

One of the most successful buy-and-hold investors of our time, Warren Buffett, likes to say that he is not buying a stock; he is buying a business. He buys stocks for the best price he can and holds them as long as he can.

Keep in mind, however, that Buffett buys stocks in conservative (some would say dull) corporations like insurance companies and banks and rarely buys technology stocks. Buffett became a billionaire using his long-term buy-and-hold investment *strategy* (a strategy is a plan that helps an investor determine which stocks to buy or sell).

Investors who bought and held shares of stock in Home Depot, Walmart, and the 3M Company saw the value of their investments increase over time.

In fact, there were many periods in the past where it was profitable to be an investor. During those years, the stock market went up by huge amounts, and some stocks doubled or tripled in price. That's as sweet as it gets for investors.

Unfortunately, there are also times when it's unprofitable to be an investor (usually during *bear markets*, when the market generally goes down). During these times, it's possible for a year's worth of gains to be erased within weeks because stock prices fall faster than they rise. Fortunately for investors, over the long term, the market tends to go up more than it goes down.

Short-Term Traders

Unlike investors, *short-term traders* don't care about the long-term prospects of a corporation. Their goal is to take advantage of the short-term movements in price. This means that they may buy and then sell a stock within five minutes, a few hours or days, or occasionally a month. Today, *high-frequency traders* (HFTs) hold stocks for microseconds. Traders are focused on the price of a stock, not on the business of the corporation.

There are many kinds of short-term traders. Trading strategies include *position trading* (holding for a month or two), *swing trading* (holding for a week until a price target is reached), and *day trading* (holding no longer than a day). Day traders buy stocks and sell them quickly (hopefully for a higher price), but always before the market closes for the day. Generally, they move all their money back to cash by the end of the day.

Professional Traders

Professional traders use other people's money (and sometimes their own) to make investments or trades on behalf of clients. Professionals include institutional traders such as pension funds, banks, brokerage firms, mutual fund companies, and hedge funds (you will learn more about institutional investors later in this book).

Institutional investors have access to billions of dollars, and they can influence not only the price of individual stocks but the entire market. Some of these institutions have set up computer programs that automatically buy or sell stocks when certain conditions are met. As mentioned earlier, high-frequency traders use computer algorithms to make thousands of trades per second in order to capture a fraction of a penny in profits. Those fractions add up to huge profits each day.

It is estimated that professional traders make up approximately 90 percent of the daily *volume* of the market, with retail investors making up the other 10 percent.

How Wall Street Keeps Score

Wall Street has several ways to keep track of the market. One of the easiest ways to find out how the market is performing during the day is to look online with a computer or mobile device. You can also follow the market by reading a newspaper, watching television, or listening to the radio.

When you hear people talk about "the market," they are usually referring to the Dow Jones Industrial Average (DJIA), which includes 30 large, well-known U.S. companies. So if you want to know if the market is up or down for the day, more than likely, you will look at the Dow Jones Industrial Average.

Note: A list of the 30 stocks in the Dow Jones Industrial Average is at the end of this chapter.

Other Indexes: S&P 500, Nasdaq, and Russell 2000

Although the Dow (operated by the *Wall Street Journal*) was the first index to keep track of stocks, hundreds of other indexes have been created to track almost everything from transportation to utilities to technology stocks. Some sophisticated investors keep an eye on many of these indexes, but most individual investors watch just four.

The next most popular index (after the Dow) is the S&P 500, primarily because it is representative of the entire U.S. stock market. If you guessed that this index contains 500 stocks, you are right. These are 500 stocks that have the largest *market capitalization*. In other words, unlike the Dow Jones Industrial Average, which is price-weighted, each stock in the S&P 500 index is assigned a weighting based on its total market capitalization. Note: I'll discuss market capitalization in Chapter 2.

The next most popular index is the Nasdaq Composite Index, which tracks all the stocks traded on the Nasdaq exchange (more than 3,000). Whenever you see the Dow listed, you will almost always see the Nasdaq below it. Other popular indexes are the Russell 2000 index and the Wilshire 5000. You'll learn later that there are ways for you to mimic the performance of the indexes, even though they cannot be bought and sold like stocks.

If you were a professional money manager, your goal each year would be to beat the major indexes. What does this mean? It means that if the Dow is up 15 percent this year, you would have to earn 15 percent or more. (Your year-end bonus depends on it.)

The bad news is that it's very hard for people, even professional investors, to beat the indexes. In fact, it's reported that more than 80 percent of the professional managers do not beat the indexes each year. In some years, only 15 or 20 percent of professional managers and hedge funds beat the S&P 500 index, and in some stock categories (such as international stock funds), even fewer beat the indexes. It is safe to say that most professional fund managers do not beat the major indexes consistently.

You can look at this statistic in three ways. First, if a professional investor can't beat the indexes, then what are your chances? Second, you might believe that you can learn to do better than the pros, which is possible but difficult. And third, you could think that investing directly in the indexes is the easiest way to match the returns of the major market indexes. (Later, I'll tell you what I think.)

In this book, I discuss all the strategies the pros use, including how to invest in the major indexes.

It's All About Points

To measure how much you make or lose in the stock market, Wall Street uses the term *points* to represent dollars. First, remember that we talked about stock shares, which is a piece of the company. You can buy 1 share, 100 shares, 1,000 shares, or as many as you can afford. And each stock has its own price, from a few pennies to a few hundred or even thousands of dollars. These prices are constantly changing.

Now, let's see how to keep score. For example, let's say you bought a stock that was selling for $20 per share. If your stock price went from $20 per share to $25 per share, your stock went up 5 points. That's the same as $5 per share. That's how we keep score on Wall Street.

Another example: If your stock went from $10 per share to $11 per share, you made one point (or one dollar for every share owned).

The same type of scoring is done with the major indexes like the Dow, the Nasdaq, and the S&P 500. If the Dow went from 15,000 to 15,100, you would say the market went up by 100 points.

Note: Although it's okay to tell people how many points you made or your percentage gain, it's not polite to tell people the exact sum you made in the markets. Even if you made $5,000 in a single day, it's best to keep it to yourself. (I'm not an etiquette expert, so use your own judgment.)

How Much Does It Cost?

If you can figure out the following calculation, then you will understand how to buy or sell stocks. Just as in an auction, every trade occurs at a specific price. This price changes frequently—several times per second for some stocks. Let's say that a stock you're interested in, YYY Manufacturing Company, is currently trading for $20 per share.

You decide that you want to buy 100 shares. The math goes like this: 100 shares multiplied by $20 per share costs $2,000. This means that you must pay $2,000 to your brokerage firm if you want to buy 100 shares of YYY.

Learning the math is easy, but to be sure you understand, here's another example. Let's say that you want to buy 1,000 shares of a stock that is selling for $15 per share. How much will it cost? The answer is $15,000. One more example: Let's say you want to buy 100 shares of a stock that costs $5 per share. It costs $500 to buy that stock.

Note: Typically, most of the stocks retail investors buy range in price from $5 to $200 per share, but that varies depending on the individual.

How Much Did You Make?

Let's say that you decide to buy 100 shares of a stock that costs $15 per share. You already know it will cost you $1,500. If the stock goes to $16, you earn 1 point. If the stock goes to $17, you make 2 points.

Here's the important part: If you have 100 shares of a stock and you made 1 point, you made $100 in profit. If the stock goes up 2 points, you made $200 in profit. So the more shares you own, the more money you'll make (or lose when the stock declines).

> *Question from a reader:* What happens if no one wants to buy my stock?
>
> *Answer:* This is actually a great question. It's like having a house sale that no one goes to. To solve this problem, the stock exchanges have set up a system in which there is always a *market maker* or specialist; in other words, there will always be someone who has a responsibility to maintain a fair and orderly market. When there are no buyers, that person steps in to buy. Where there are no sellers, that person steps in to sell. You may not get the best price, but at least you know that there is someone who is willing to buy or sell stock.

I'll discuss the role of the market maker and specialist now.

Specialists

On the NYSE, the *specialist* acts as the intermediary for each stock. The specialists "make a market" for one or a few different stocks, and there are enough specialists to cover all stocks that are listed on the exchange. This means that specialists keep track of the transactions and work to get buyers and sellers together. Sometimes specialists use their own money if no one else wants to buy or sell the stock. Does this sound like a fun job? Computers and mobile devices do most of the work now. Before computers, the specialists used to fill the orders manually, one at a time. Once orders increased from hundreds to billions of shares, computers were installed to handle the orders.

You might wonder how the specialists get paid, since they often use their own money to fill the orders. First of all, no one pays the market makers. They run a business based on their individual profits and losses. They do unwanted trades to keep the markets orderly, but they are entitled to buy and sell to manage their own risk. Specialists also make money by maintaining a market. This compensates them for the risk they take when they use their own money to buy or sell.

If you are buying only a few hundred shares or even a few thousand, it's not worth your time to worry too much about whether the specialists are prospering. They do not care about your order, no matter how many shares you trade.

Market Makers

At the Nasdaq market, the computerized stock exchange, market makers match buyers and sellers. Market makers are individuals or firms that are obligated to buy and sell stocks during the trading day. It is the market maker's job to provide *liquidity* in the marketplace, which describes how easy it is to buy or sell a stock. (The more liquidity, the better.)

The main job of the market maker is to keep the market moving or flowing in order to maintain a fair and orderly market. Because of hand-held computers and mobile devices, there are fewer individual market makers than there were in the past. Most of the liquidity is managed by computers, which automatically buy and sell stocks on behalf of the market maker firms.

Unlike the arrangement at the NYSE, where only one specialist is assigned to a stock, at the Nasdaq you can have multiple market makers for a stock. The more popular the stock, the more market makers will be assigned to it.

For instance, a stock like Apple could have as many as 30 market makers, while a $1 stock with low trading volume might have only one market maker. There is, however, at least one market maker assigned to each Nasdaq stock. Keep in mind that all this happens behind the scenes within seconds. Because billions of shares are traded each day, your orders end up being routed by computers. It is nice to know, however, that there will always be someone who is willing to buy or sell shares of your stock.

And now, let's take a look at the three directions that stocks can go: up, down, or sideways. In fact, one of the reasons that stocks are easy to understand is they can only go in one of these three directions.

Bull Market: When the Market Goes Up

Bull markets are very profitable for most traders and investors. During a bull market, Wall Street is pleased because investors are putting more money into the market, and money managers receive huge bonuses. Individual investors are pleased because the value of their 401(k)s and IRAs is rising, and this makes them feel rich. Also, businesses are pleased because consumers feel wealthier, and spend more freely.

In a bull market, everyone seems to be in a stock-buying mood, often for no reason except that everyone else seems to be buying. During these times, the major indexes have nowhere to go but up. People are optimistic about the direction of the country, and people are talking about how much money they made in the market.

In the early 1920s, the bull market was fueled by the increased popularity of automobiles and electricity. In the bull market of the 1990s, the Internet drove stock prices higher. At the beginning of the twenty-first century, after two stock market crashes (in 2001 and 2008), a great bull market was fueled by a cooperative Federal Reserve, increased optimism about the U.S. economy, and low interest rates.

Important: Bull and bear markets are part of a *market cycle.* The market can't keep going up forever, nor will it go down forever. But in the past, bear markets have been relatively short (no longer than a year), while bull markets can last as long as three or four years. Unfortunately, every bull and bear market is different, so it's hard to predict exactly how long one may last.

During many bull markets, investors think that the good times will last forever. You know it's a bull market when negative news is ignored, and the market goes higher. Investors continue buying stocks based on the fear of missing out on a continued rally. Stock prices keep rising and the market seems unstoppable.

Bear Market: When Stocks Go Down

Sometimes the market goes through a period of several months (or longer) when it keeps going down. That has happened a number of times in the history of the stock market. When the stock market is officially in a bear market (the market decline is more than 20 percent), it means that the major market indexes—the Dow, Nasdaq, and S&P 500—are plunging. People may panic and sell their stocks for whatever price they can get. Others may hold on, trapped and confused about what to do next. In general, the economy is weak, and corporate earnings are declining.

A bear market is pretty depressing for Wall Street. People tend to avoid the stock market and put their money in cash, gold, or bonds. On Wall Street, the major brokerages stop hiring or they lay off employees. Even when a company releases positive news, in a bear market stocks might remain unchanged or even drop in price.

Since the stock market often predicts what will happen to the economy, a lengthy bear market may signal that a recession is coming or has already arrived. No one can predict how long a bear market will last, although bear markets in the past have been relatively short.

Note: A *market correction*, on the other hand, occurs when the market plunges, but less than 20 percent.

Sideways Market: When the Market Goes Nowhere

Wall Street dreads a sideways market because it's hard to make money when there are no customers to buy stocks. In a sideways market, the market attempts to go up or down but ends up just about where it started. Investors may sit on the sidelines, holding their cash and refusing to participate in the market, earning nothing.

One of the longest sideways markets occurred after the 1929 stock market crash. After reaching a low in 1932, it took another 22 years for the market to return to its 1929 high of 381 for the Dow (and that is not a typo).

During a sideways market, neither the bulls nor bears make money (although short-term traders can find opportunities). In fact, it takes a lot of patience to invest during a sideways market because profits are often elusive.

Bottom line: Before placing your first penny in the market, be prepared for any possibility: a bull, bear, or sideways market. Note: In this book, I show you strategies you can use during all market types.

How the Dow Jones Industrial Average Was Created

In 1884, a reporter named Charles Dow calculated an average of the closing prices of 11 railroad stocks. His goal was to find a way to measure how the stock market did each day. He then wrote comments about the stock market in a four-page daily newspaper called a "flimsie," which became the *Wall Street Journal.*

A few years later, the company Charles Dow helped start, Dow Jones, launched the Dow Jones Industrial Average, consisting of 12 industrial stocks. If you know about averages, you know that you basically add up the prices of the stocks in the index and divide by the number of stocks to calculate the daily average. By watching the Dow, you can get a general idea of how the market is doing. It also gives us clues to the *trend* of the market, whether it is going up, down, or sideways. (The trend is simply the direction in which a stock or market is going.)

The original 12 stocks in the Dow were the biggest and most popular companies at the end of the nineteenth century—for example, American Tobacco, Distilling and Cattle Feeding, U.S. Leather, and General Electric, to name a few. Guess which stock still remains in the index? (If you guessed General Electric, you are right. The other corporations either went out of business or merged with other corporations.)

By 1928, the Dow Jones Industrial Average had increased to 30 stocks, which is the number of stocks in the index today. (By the way, this index is sometimes called *the Dow 30*.) These 30 stocks are a cross section of the most important industrial *sectors* in the stock market. (A sector is a group of companies in the same industry, such as technology, utilities, energy, biomedical, etc.)

The Dow is a price-weighted index, which means that stocks with a higher weighting affect the Dow index more than stocks with a lower weighting. For example, since IBM is weighted high in today's market (because of its high stock price), when this stock is having a bad day and falls by several points, the Dow is very likely to be down for the day even when none of the other stocks declines.

It's easy to find out how the Dow did each day—it's reported online, on TV, and just about everywhere. Since more than half of the public is invested in the stock market, there is a lot of interest in what the Dow does each day. Therefore, when we talk about the Dow Jones being up or down, we're really talking about a representative group of 30 stocks, the Dow 30. Even if the market declines, the stock you own could be up, or the other way around.

Here is a list of the Dow 30 stocks (including the *ticker symbol*, which is a unique letter code that is used to identify each stock.

3M Company (MMM)
American Express (AXP)
Amgen, Inc. (AMGN)
Apple, Inc. (AAPL)
Boeing Company (BA)
Caterpillar, Inc. (CAT)
Chevron Corporation (CVX)
Cisco Systems, Inc. (CSCO)
Coca-Cola (KO)
Dow, Inc. (DOW)
Goldman Sachs (GS)
Home Depot, Inc. (HD)
Honeywell International, Inc. (HON)
Intel Corporation (INTC)
International Business Machines (IBM)
Johnson & Johnson (JNJ)
JPMorgan Chase and Co. (JPM)
McDonald's Corp. (MCD)
Merck & Co. Inc. (MRK)
Microsoft Corp. (MSFT)
Nike (NKE)
Procter & Gamble (PG)
Salesforce.com, Inc. (CRM)
Travelers Companies Inc. (TRV)
UnitedHealth Group Inc. (UNH)
Verizon Communications Inc. (VZ)
Visa (V)
Walgreens Boots Alliance, Inc. (WBA)
Walmart Stores (WMT)
Walt Disney Company (DIS)

Note: On occasion, stocks are added to or removed from the Dow 30.

Perhaps you're already thinking you'd like to open a broker-age account and start investing. Be patient. It is essential to learn more before you place your money at risk. The biggest mistake you can make is to enter the market with too much money and too little knowledge.

· ·

And now, let's learn about the different ways you can classify stocks.

2

Classifying Stocks: Value, Income, and Growth

If you want to understand the stock market, you should learn the different ways in which people classify and identify stocks. In fact, stocks are often identified by their *sector* or *industry*.

Stock Sectors

As mentioned earlier, a *sector* is a group of companies that loosely belongs to the same industry and provides similar products or services. Examples of stock sectors include airlines, software, chemicals, oil, retail, automobiles, and pharmaceuticals. Understanding sectors is important if you want to make money in the stock market. The reason is simple: No matter how the market is doing and no matter what the condition of the economy, there are always sectors that are doing well and sectors that are struggling.

For example, during bear markets, the computer and technology sectors and anything related to the Internet (i.e., growth stocks) often get hit the hardest. Many pros shift their money out of the weak sectors and move into "recession-proof" sectors such as food, pharmaceuticals, beverages, and household goods (i.e., consumer staples).

Even in a recession, people must eat, drink, take medicines, and buy household goods such as tissue and toilet paper.

Some professional traders shift their money into and out of sectors every day. Once they identify the strongest sectors for the day using charts, they pick what they think is the strongest stock in that sector.

Like anything connected to the stock market, successfully shifting into and out of sectors sounds easier to accomplish than it is in real life, and is best left to the pros. It's always easier to look in the rearview mirror to figure out what sectors were most profitable. Nevertheless, it's worth taking the time to understand and identify the various sectors and to be aware of which sectors are strong and which are weak.

Classifying Stocks by Earnings Growth

In addition to identifying stocks by sectors, you can also classify stocks by how much their earnings have grown in the past, and thus are expected to grow in the future. The three main types of stocks are value, income, and growth.

Value Stocks: Stocks That Sell for Less than They're Worth

Value stocks are shares of companies that are selling at a reasonable price compared with their true worth, or value. The trick, of course, is determining what a company is really worth. The goal is to find solid stocks that are undervalued. Some low-priced stocks that seem like bargains might be costly, while a high-priced stock might actually be a bargain. Just knowing the price of a stock isn't enough. You also have to know what it's worth. To paraphrase Oscar Wilde, too many people know the price of everything but the value of nothing.

Value stocks are often those of old-fashioned companies, such as insurance companies, retail stores, and certain banks, that are likely to increase in price in the future. It takes a lot of research to find a company whose price is a bargain compared to its value. Investors who are attracted to value stocks use a number of fundamental tools to find these bargain stocks. (I discuss many of these tools in Chapter 11.)

Income Stocks: A Conservative Way to Make Money

Income stocks include shares of corporations that give money back to shareholders in the form of *dividends* (some people call these stocks *dividend stocks*). Some investors, usually those who don't like taking risks, like dividends because they provide a cash return on their investment dollars. Investors who are near retirement are also attracted to income stocks because they plan to live off the income. This is another way for investors to share in the company's profits.

Stocks that pay a regular dividend tend to be less *volatile* (the price does not rise or fall as quickly) than others, which is fine with the conservative investors who buy income stocks. Another advantage is that the dividends reduce the loss if the stock price goes down. Income stocks can be in any sector, but typically they are in industries such as energy, utilities, and natural resources.

There are also a few disadvantages to buying income stocks. First, dividends are considered taxable income, so you have to report the income to the IRS. Second, if the company doesn't raise its dividend each year—and many don't—inflation can cut into your returns. Finally, income stocks can fall, even if not as quickly as other stocks. Just because you own stock in a so-called conservative company doesn't mean that you will be protected against losing money if the stock market falls.

Growth Stocks: Volatile Stocks Fueled by Strong Earnings

Growth stocks are the stocks of companies that consistently grow their earnings year after year. They are expected to grow faster than the competition, and the stock price reflects that expectation. Strong earnings, and the acceleration of those earnings, make growth stocks attractive for investors. These stocks are often in high-tech industries.

Sometimes, the price of growth stocks can be extremely high with a high *price-to-earnings* ratio (P/E), especially when the company's earnings aren't spectacular. This is because growth investors believe that the corporation will earn money in the future so they are willing to invest now. However, even one disappointing earnings report can cause the stock to decline quickly.

Because growth stocks can be volatile, they can be risky investments. These are ideal for short-term traders who want to play for a quick profit, or for long-term investors who believe in the company and its business model. The volatility, however, is unnerving for many.

Note: The P/E ratio and other fundamental tools will be discussed in Chapter 12.

Classifying Stocks by Size

You can also classify stocks by size. The *market capitalization* (or *market cap*) of a stock tells you how large the corporation is. To calculate market cap, multiply the number of *outstanding shares* (which is easily found online) by the current stock price. For example, a large corporation with one billion outstanding shares and a stock price of $50 has a market cap of $50 billion.

Some people will invest only in *large-cap stocks* (those of large corporations worth over $10 billion), including the stocks of corporations such as Coca-Cola, Home Depot, and Johnson & Johnson. Why? They feel that the stocks of these corporations are safer to own and will not tumble in price. (*Note:* Thanks to companies like Lehman Brothers and Enron, we know that even large, well-known corporations can go bankrupt.)

Other investors are attracted to *mid-cap stocks* (those of medium-sized corporations worth between $2 and $10 billion), while still others invest in *small-cap* or *microcap* stocks (those of small corporations worth between $300 million and $2 billion) because their price often moves quickly.

It's not easy for large-cap stocks to double or triple in price. For example, for the stock price of a large-cap stock to double from $50 to $100, the company would have to increase in value from $100 billion to $200 billion—not impossible, but extremely difficult. Some investors prefer nimble small-cap stocks because there is a better chance that they will double or triple in value. On the other hand, smaller-cap stocks come with a higher risk that the business will fail. Buying stock in very small companies is an example of taking more risk to seek a higher profit.

Outstanding Shares

Outstanding shares are the total number of shares that a corporation has issued. This also includes shares that are held by company insiders and officers.

It's up to the board of directors of corporations to decide how many shares are issued and what is done with the shares. Obviously, the board keeps shares of the stock for the company's officers and employees.

The number of outstanding shares is listed on a company's balance sheet. You can also find the number of outstanding shares on Google Finance, Yahoo! Finance, and Value Line, but there are other websites.

Why is it important to know about outstanding shares? When you learn how to analyze stocks in Chapter 11, the number of outstanding shares is used to calculate a company's earnings, as well as the market capitalization.

Dividends: Another Way to Make Money

You already know that many investors are attracted to income stocks because these stocks pay dividends. Let's take a closer look at exactly how dividends work.

As mentioned before, a corporation that earns money may pass some of those profits to shareholders in the form of a payment called a dividend. The payment is usually given to shareholders in cash, and some companies make it easy to reinvest those dividends.

Collecting dividends is a great idea. The investor receives part of the company profits in cash. For those interested in building wealth over time, you can use those dividends to buy more shares. Keep in mind that the corporation's board of directors is not required to distribute a dividend but does so when dividends fit into the company business plan.

Dividends are not free money because the price of the stock declines by the amount of the dividend (which occurs on the *ex-dividend day*. The dividend is paid to people who already own the stock prior to the ex-dividend day).

No matter how many shares you own, those quarterly dividend payments can help build wealth over the years. Many people like stocks that pay dividends, especially investors who are nearing retirement age because they can depend on those dividend checks to live. The corporations that traditionally pay dividends are the large blue-chip companies that are included in the Dow Jones Industrial Average (in the game of poker, *blue chips* are the most valuable).

Sometimes corporations, even the blue chips, decide to lower or eliminate their dividends. A dividend increase is typically a positive event, and often the stock price increases. On the other hand, a dividend cut may mean that the business is not doing well and the company cannot afford to pay those dividends. Often, the stock price falls after a dividend cut.

By the way, you can easily find out the dividend payment, if any, that a corporation pays by looking online or in a financial newspaper.

. . . .

Now that you know how to classify stocks, let's take a look at other fun things you can do with stocks.

3

Fun Things You Can Do
(with Stocks)

In this chapter, you will learn about diversification, allocation, compounding, and stock splits. Let's look at each of these concepts one by one.

Diversification: Avoid Putting All Your Eggs in One Basket

One way to reduce risk is by *diversification*, so instead of betting your entire *portfolio* on one or two stocks, you spread the risk by investing in a variety of securities. (A portfolio is made up of securities, including stocks, mutual funds, bonds, and cash equivalents, that you own. You will learn about these products in Chapter 8.) The idea behind diversification is that even if one or two investments go sour, your other investments can make up the losses.

At the most basic level, if you put all your money in one stock, you could either earn a windfall or suffer a harmful loss. For example, one of my neighbors put all his money in a top technology stock, one of the best companies in the world. After 10 years of buy and hold investing his portfolio was valued at over $800,000.

Instead of selling half or even some shares, he held onto his shares even as the stock went lower and lower. He lost his house, filed for divorce, and never recovered financially or psychologically. So if you ask me whether you should diversify, I suggest that you do.

In addition, some people invest all their money in the stock of the company they work for. This is not always wise. If the company runs into difficulty, you could lose money as well as your job.

Note: Some companies offer employee stock purchase programs (ESPPs), allowing you to buy stock in the company at a discount. In my opinion, this is an excellent way of building wealth through the stock market, especially if you work for a quality company with growing earnings. Nevertheless, at some point it makes sense to diversify your holdings by selling some of that stock.

Here's how diversification works. Let's say that you are 100 percent invested (i.e., all of your investable cash is in the stock market). To be fully diversified, you need at least 5 to 10 stocks in various industries. Later you'll learn about *mutual funds* and *exchange-traded funds (ETFs)*, which provide instant diversification.

Many financial experts suggest that you own a mixture of growth, value, and income stocks, along with a smattering of international stocks. You might also consider stocks in both large and small companies.

Diversification can be confusing. To do it properly, you need to consider how much risk you are comfortable taking (called *risk tolerance*), your age, your time horizon, and your investment goals. Many suggest that you simply buy stocks and bonds (we discuss bonds in Chapter 15), but doing this doesn't always make sense.

Truthfully, it takes an understanding of how and why diversification works to diversify properly. A mistake that many people make is putting all their money in one sector such as technology and incorrectly thinking that they are diversified. Although putting all your investment dollars in one sector can bring huge profits if you're right, if you're wrong (as my neighbor was), you could be hurt badly.

Note: Some people hire *financial planners* to help with the diversification process. Only you can decide whether this is an appropriate path for your assets. On the one hand, you want to be properly diversified so you aren't exposed to too much risk. On the other hand, you don't want to be overdiversified (i.e., when you own so many stocks, mutual funds, or ETFs that it's difficult for these to outperform market averages).

Asset Allocation: Deciding How Much Money to Allot to Each Investment

Once you have a diversified portfolio, you have to decide what percentage of your money you want to allocate (or distribute) to each investment. For example, if you are 30 years away from retirement, you could invest 65 percent in individual stocks and mutual funds and 25 percent in bonds, and keep 10 percent in cash. This is an example of asset allocation.

In the old days, you were told to subtract your age from 100 to determine the percentage of your assets to put into stocks. For example, if you are 40 years old, 100 minus 40 equals 60. This old formula suggests that you invest 60 percent in stocks and 40 percent in bonds.

The problem with this formula is that it is too conservative and you could easily outlive your money. In addition, a severe market correction can take all assets down together.

Bottom line: You want to be properly diversified. Unfortunately, what is considered "proper" for one person may not work for you in the real world. Understanding diversification and asset allocation takes time. You will learn later that there are certain investments, such as index funds and mutual funds, that provide instant diversification.

Compounding: Creating Earnings on Your Earnings

There is something you can do with stocks that can make you rich, that is, if you are a patient investor. It's called *compound interest*, and Einstein once wrote that it "was the eighth wonder of the world. He who understands it, earns it. He who doesn't ... pays it." The idea behind compound interest is one reason why people reinvest any profits and dividends.

Compounding works like this: You reinvest all earnings from your investments: interest, dividends, or capital gains. The longer you keep reinvesting your earnings, the more money you'll make. In other words, you earn money on the profits and not only on the original investment. If compounding is new to you, the numbers can be an eye-opener.

For example, if you invest $100 and it grows by 10 percent in one year, at the end of the year you'll have a total of $110. If you reinvest that $10, you'll have $121 by the end of the next year. $10 would represent your regular earnings, but that extra $1 comes from *compounded earnings,* or the earnings that are earned on the first year's $10 earnings. It may not seem like much extra money, but compounding year after year makes a huge difference. The more your investment is earning, the faster it compounds. The advocates of compounding remind you to invest early if you want to have more money later. Believe them, because it is true. You are never too young to begin.

Compounding is a neat strategy that can make you rich if you begin early in life. The idea is that as the stocks you own increase in value, your earnings (trading profits and dividends) compound as you continuously invest by buying more shares. This brings greater profits. The longer you leave your money in any investment, the more powerful compounding becomes. John Bogle, founder and the former chairman of the mutual fund company Vanguard, called compounding "the greatest mathematical discovery of all time for the investor seeking maximum reward." Investors who believe in buying and holding stocks often mention the power of compounding over the long term.

Compounding formulas work like a charm as long as your investment increases in value. The problem with the stock market is that there are no guarantees that your stock will go up in price or that you'll make a specific return each year in the market.

Stock Splits: Convincing People to Buy Your Stock

A *stock split* occurs when the board of directors at a company decides to issue more shares of stock to shareholders. For example, if a corporation announces a 2-for-1 stock split, it doubles the number of shares in existence, so every shareholder receives one extra share for every share held. This is not a windfall. The company is worth exactly what it was worth before the stock split. As a result, you will own twice as many shares, each worth one-half of the original shares. There is no economic gain, but market participants tend to like stock splits. Sometimes, the stock price increases when a split is announced.

From a mathematical perspective, nothing has changed. You own twice as many shares, but since the stock price was reduced by half, the value of your investment is exactly the same. (*Note:* You can also have a 3-for-1, 4-for-1, or even a 3-for-2 stock split.)

A stock split is often done for psychological reasons more than anything else. In reality, a stock split doesn't change the corporation's financial condition. Instead, the biggest advantage of a stock split is that it may bring in more investors—those who felt that they couldn't afford to buy stock at a higher price.

Nevertheless, there are practical reasons for a company to split its stock. For example, do you know what would happen if a corporation never split its stock? Think about Berkshire Hathaway, Warren Buffett's corporation. At one time, his stock was trading at over $160,000 per share. That is not a typo! Many people couldn't afford even one share of stock at that price.

So from a practical standpoint, stock splits do make sense for some corporations. Splitting the stock is purely an accounting (or marketing) procedure designed to make a stock more enticing to investors. It does not increase the value of the corporation.

Note: Some companies do a reverse split, when the stock price is too low, where they reduce the number of shares outstanding. Reverse splits are often done for psychological reasons to boost shareholder confidence. For example, to pump up the stock price, the board of directors might do a 1:10 (one for ten) reverse split. After the reverse split, the value of your shares remains the same, but you own fewer shares. If a company does a reverse split, it's a warning sign, and is typically done when the stock price has already declined a lot. If a company does a reverse spilt, and is artificially raising the stock price, it might be time to think about selling, a decision only you can make.

· ·

In the next chapter, you will learn how to open a brokerage account so you can buy and sell stocks.

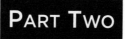

PART TWO

HOW TO ENTER, EXIT, AND ESCAPE STOCKS

Opening a Brokerage Account

Many of you are eager to get started investing, and in this chapter, I show you how to open a brokerage account. As I said before, opening and funding an account is the fun part. Before you invest real money, however, I suggest that you read the entire book.

And now I'll take you through the steps of opening a brokerage account.

Step 1: Choose a Brokerage Firm

The first thing you must do is to select a brokerage firm. This is an important decision because if you pick the wrong firm, it can cost money in unnecessary fees, commissions, and poor order fills.

There are three main types of brokerage firms, which I explain in detail.

Online Brokerage Firms

Online brokerage firms, which used to be called discount brokers, are ideal for independent investors and traders. *Online investing* or *online trading* simply means that you enter orders to buy and sell online from your own computer or mobile device. (You can also invest in bonds, mutual funds, ETFs, and fixed-income products like CDs and Treasuries.)

The best online brokerage firms have a nationally known reputation, a 12-hour help desk to answer any questions, and simple screens.

Fortunately, almost all online brokerage firms have representatives who answer your questions and guide you through their screens. As long as you decide what to buy and sell, many online firms should meet your needs.

Online brokerage firms have streaming real-time quotes and easy-to-navigate and secure websites. Most online firms also have educational resources such as articles, webinars, and information about investing and trading strategies. The top firms also offer research with sophisticated charts, trading alerts, customizable screens, and profit-and-loss screens.

The downside to opening an account with an online brokerage is that online firms offer little or no investment advice. If you feel that investment advice is needed or if you have a huge portfolio that is difficult to manage, an online broker might not be right for you. That is a decision only you can make, however.

Where can you find a current list of the top-rated online brokerage firms? Go to any search engine and type: "Rank online brokerage firms," followed by the current year. A list of articles will appear from independent sources such as *Barron's,* Investopedia, or MarketWatch.

Full-Service Brokerage Firm: Bells and Whistles for a Steep Price

Full-service brokerage firms include some of the largest and most influential stock brokerage firms on Wall Street. These brokerage firms provide a variety of banking and investment products geared primarily to a wealthy clientele who don't have the time or desire to manage their own accounts. Unless you have a huge portfolio, don't expect to receive a high level of personalized service.

If you open an account with a full-service brokerage firm, you will be assigned a person to handle your account. Such people used to be called stockbrokers, but because unscrupulous brokers gave the industry a bad reputation, stockbrokers now refer to themselves using a variety of creative names, such as financial consultants, account executives, or investment managers.

Stockbrokers not only are paid to offer advice on buying and selling decisions, but they also see that your orders are executed. For this service, they are paid a commission on each trade.

The problem with the commission-based system is that it's in the broker's best interest to direct you toward buying in-house products (such as the firm's mutual funds), because those provide the highest commissions. In addition, some unethical brokers "churn" your account (make far more trades than necessary).

If you do hire a stockbroker at a full-service brokerage firm, my advice is to find an honest, competent individual who truly cares about your investment portfolio. What you don't need is a fast-talking salesperson who wants to make money for himself or herself by generating bigger commissions.

Often, stockbrokers at these firms know little about buying and selling stocks and are only salespeople who recommend stocks in companies that they represent. These are the stocks they want you to buy, along with their in-house funds. Ironically, they are trained to tell you that retail customers have no business buying and selling stocks on their own. "Let us do all the work so you can go to the beach," is the message they want to give you.

In response to complaints about the commission-based system, some brokerages have changed their fee structure for clients with large portfolios. Instead of charging commissions on each trade, some charge a 1 or 2 percent annual fee. In the end, it is really your choice whether a full-service stock brokerage meets your needs.

In my opinion, many full-service brokerage firms are more interested in keeping your money than in making you money. If you do open an account with one of these firms, monitor your account closely for excessive fees and commissions, and don't let them make decisions without your final approval.

One of the reasons you are reading this book is so you don't have to rely on stockbrokers at full-service brokerage firms to make the buying and selling decisions for you. Even if someone else is managing your account, it's important that you know how to monitor your own investments.

An example of a full-service brokerage firm is Lehman Brothers: once the fourth largest investment bank, it ultimately went bankrupt.

Money Managers

If you have a large portfolio (at least $500,000), you can hire a *money manager*. For a fee, usually 1 to 2 percent of assets per year, he or she will manage your entire portfolio. This person will buy and sell the stocks, bonds, or other securities, and all you do is pay a quarterly fee.

If you find a trustworthy and competent firm, money managers can increase the value of your portfolio. If you do not feel comfortable managing your own account, there are competent money managers, but they are not easy to find, nor do most of them consistently beat the market.

Rely on word of mouth and do your own independent research to find a money manager. Most important, no matter whom you choose, be sure that you remain in control. Fraudster Bernard Madoff got away with his Ponzi scheme for over 20 years because he controlled all his clients' money. If someone asked too many questions, he'd either give a vague answer or refuse to accept that person's money.

There are a lot of lessons to be learned from the Madoff scandal. No matter whom you choose to do business with, ask questions, and insist on looking at the buy and sell transactions. Anyone can make money when the market is going up (bull market), but how did this person do in a bear market? After reading this book, you will think of many questions. An honest, competent money manager will answer them all.

After getting caught, Madoff had some advice for investors. He said that if you hire a money manager, make sure the manager uses an independent *custodian* (a financial institution such as a bank or brokerage that holds client assets), and also a qualified auditor, adding essential layers of security.

Bottom line: Since you are reading this book, I assume that you will open and manage an account with an online brokerage firm, so let's get started.

Step 2: Opening an Online Account

After you choose an online brokerage firm, you can contact the firm in person (if it has local offices), on the phone, or online. If you ask, it will send you an enrollment packet via e-mail or by mail. You can also enroll on the phone and sign the forms electronically.

Everyone wants to know how much money is needed to get started. You can open an online account with an online trading brokerage for as little as a few hundred dollars, but some require a minimum of $2,500. Call and find out the minimum required.

After enrolling, write a check to fund the account. You might also have to fill out a questionnaire that asks about your investment experience and risk tolerance. Don't be concerned with your answers; it's not a test, and it isn't used for anything. (In fact, after you make your first investment, the questionnaire is filed away and probably never looked at again.)

The check you sent to the brokerage firm is usually put into a cash account, which is similar to a savings account (it could also be a money market account). After you are "funded," the hard work begins. Although buying and selling stocks is easy, making a profit is hard work. If you've never invested in the market before, there is no need to rush. Right now, it's more important that you learn about the market. The stock market will still be there when you're ready to invest.

When you open up an account, you will be asked whether you want to have a *margin* or cash account. With a margin account, you can borrow money from your brokerage firm, which allows you to invest additional money in the same (or a different) stock.

Usually, the brokerage will give you a 2-to-1 margin rate. For example, if you have $2,500 in your account to buy shares of XYZ, the brokerage will lend you up to an additional $2,500, allowing you to invest a total of $5,000. You will be charged a competitive interest rate on the borrowed $2,500.

The advantage of margin is that you are using the brokerage firm's money to make more money (this is called *leverage*). Leveraging works great if your investment increases in value. On the other hand, if your portfolio declines in value, not only do you lose some or all of your original investment (which is painful enough), but you'll still owe all the money that you borrowed. In the stock market, stocks go down faster than they go up, so margin adds extra risk for investors.

If your stocks fall a lot while you are on margin, you might get the dreaded *margin call.* The broker will call, demanding that you provide more cash or equities. If you don't move fast enough, the broker has the right to sell some of your positions until the margin percentage is at the proper level (usually 30 percent or more).

Most people don't have the knowledge or discipline to handle margin correctly, which is why I think you should avoid it. In my opinion, margin is a risky tactic that is best left to experienced traders. Invest what you can afford without borrowing. If you don't heed this advice, you'll know what I mean after you receive your first margin call.

Step 3: Understanding Stock Prices

Ready to have fun? Let's say you have filled out the necessary paperwork and opened an account with an online broker. Your beginning balance is $2,500, which is sitting safely in a cash account. You are now at your computer, and you're ready to make a trade. The first thing you need to do is learn how to read a stock quote.

A stock quote (or quotation) is simply the current price of a stock. An example of a detailed stock quote for YYY is shown in Figure 4.1. It includes basic information such as the ticker symbol, bid and ask prices, volume, and the last trade. It also includes details such as shares outstanding, market capitalization, 52-week high and low, ex-dividend date and dividend pay date (if any), and the stock's one-year price performance.

Where to Find a Stock Quote

If you don't know the current price of a stock, you can quickly find it online at your brokerage firm's website or at dozens of financial sites such as Google Finance or Yahoo! Finance. You can also download apps for your mobile device to read quotes anywhere.

Each stock has it own *ticker symbol* (such as YYY). Some are easy to remember; for example, the stock symbol for IBM is IBM. The symbol for Microsoft is MSFT. AT&T is T, General Electric is GE, Alphabet is GOOG, and Apple is AAPL. If you aren't sure of the exact ticker symbol, type in the name of the company, and the ticker symbol will be displayed quickly on your computer or mobile device.

Most people refer to a stock by its symbol rather than its full name. Every experienced investor knows the ticker symbols for the most popular stocks. If the stock is on the Nasdaq, the symbol will usually have four or five letters (but not always). If the stock is on the NYSE, it will have one, two, or three letters.

> *Hint:* Type "stock quote" in your search engine and different websites will appear. In addition to your brokerage firm, three popular websites that have free real-time quotes are Yahoo! Finance, Google Finance, and Quote.com. There are dozens of other websites with this information. You can also look on financial television programs like CNBC, Bloomberg, or Fox Business News for updated quotes and financial news.

Last Trade	44.7099
Trade Time	2:29:03pm ET
Last Trade Exchange	Third Market
Today's Change	0.3499
Today's % Change	0.79%
Bid	44.67
Bid Size	1
Bid Exchange	NYSE ARCA
Ask	44.71
Ask Size	2
Ask Exchange	Direct Edge

Open	45.14
Today's High	45.56
Today's Low	43.89
Previous Close Price	44.36
52-Week High	51.939
52-Week Low	20.2467
Price Performance (Last 52 Weeks)	+109.57%

Market Capitalization	$4.42B
Shares Outstanding	99,667,000
Shares Short*	25,142,039
Short Interest as a % of Shares Outstanding*	25.23%
Days to Cover	5.93
P/E (Trailing Twelve Months)	97.84
PEG Ratio (5-Year Projected)	4.80
Ex. Dividend Date	--
Dividend Pay Date	--

Figure 4.1 Detailed stock quote

Source: Fidelity Investments.

Bid and Ask

When you look at the detailed stock quote in Figure 4.1, you will see two prices. These are the *bid price* (the lower price) and the *ask price* (the higher price). The bid and ask prices are extremely important.

All stocks have quotes: The bid price is the price at which you can sell stock, and the ask price is the price at which you can buy. To help you remember this, think of it this way: The lower number is the price you can sell, and the higher number is the price you can buy.

- *Bid:* This is the highest published price anyone is currently willing to pay if you want to sell stock.
- *Ask:* This is the lowest published price anyone is currently willing to accept if you buy stock.
- *Note:* It is not necessary to pay as high as the ask price or to sell as low as the bid price. You may enter an order at any price that suits your needs. However, the farther you move away from those bid-ask prices, the less chance that your order will be filled.

In Figure 4.1, the bid price for YYY is $44.67. The higher price is the ask price, the price you may have to pay if you want to buy this stock. The ask price for YYY is $44.71. (Remember that you don't have to enter this price, but may bid less. But if you want the order filled quickly, you can bid $44.71.)

Note: More than likely, you will buy or sell stocks at a price between the bid and ask prices. Note that the difference between the bid and ask prices is only a few pennies. This difference is called the *spread.*

The Bid-Ask Spread

As you just learned, the difference between the bid and ask prices is called the *spread.* In Figure 4.1, the difference between the bid price ($44.67) and the ask price ($44.71) is $0.04. With most stocks, the spread is only a penny or two. With stocks that are not very liquid and aren't traded often, the spread can be wide (a nickel or more).

If you see a stock with a wide spread, this is a red flag. It means that when you decide to sell at a later time, it will likely cost more money. The more narrow the spread, the better for investors.

Keep in mind that the stock quote is just a quick snapshot in time of what is happening with the stock. Although these numbers are useful, if you want to really get to know a stock, you'll have to dig deeper, as you'll learn as you read the rest of the book.

What is a Fair Price?

When you look at the stock quote, you also see data describing how much the stock has risen or fallen for the trading day in both absolute and percentage terms. In Figure 4.1, YYY is up $0.34, or 0.79 percent. Many people also look at the 52-week lows and highs to get an idea of where the stock price has been in the recent past.

As you'll learn when you continue reading, the stock price is actually a small piece of the puzzle we call the stock market. Although you must know how much a stock costs, the price doesn't tell you how much it's worth. After all, you don't want to buy a stock that is overpriced. Never forget that the stock market is like an auction, so you aim to buy stocks at a fair price and sell when the stock is higher. It's not easy to do, but that is one of your goals.

Unfortunately, many people don't realize that a stock selling for $50 can be a better value than a stock selling for $10. If a company with a $10 stock has little or no earnings and loads of debt, you'd be better off buying fewer shares of the $50 stock rather than more shares of the $10 stock. (Successful investor Warren Buffett once said, "It's far better to buy a wonderful company at a fair price than a fair company at a wonderful price.")

Now lets buy our first stock.

Buying Your First Stock

Before you buy your first stock, you need to know the vocabulary so that you will know how to place an order correctly. You have a number of order choices, and it's essential that you learn them all. It's very common for people to make mistakes when placing orders, which can cost money.

Let's say that you have decided to buy 100 shares of YYY, which is trading at $44 per share.

Note: Before you buy shares of any stock, it's suggested you do research. Where do you start? First, I suggest you not buy shares until you have read this entire book. Then you will know about the risks as well as the benefits of buying stock. Second, in Chapter 18, I list dozens of resources, including other stock market books and websites that you can view. Learning about the stock market takes a long time, so be patient. Opening a brokerage account will also help you learn about the market (but start with small sums).

To buy stock online at your brokerage firm, first enter your user ID and password (which your brokerage firm provides), and sign into your account. You'll immediately see how much money you have in your account.

In our example, you have $5,000 in your account, and you want to buy 100 shares of YYY, which last traded for $44.69. The current ask

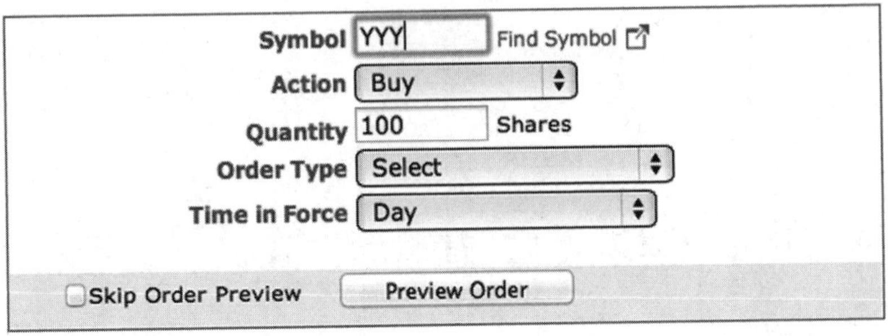

Symbol	YYY｜　　　Find Symbol 📷
Action	Buy　　　　　　　　　▲▼
Quantity	100　　　　Shares
Order Type	Select　　　　　　　▲▼
Time in Force	Day　　　　　　　　▲▼

☐Skip Order Preview　　　　　Preview Order

Figure 5.1　Order entry screen

price is $44.71 per share (ask price), and it will cost $4,471 (100 shares × $44.71 per share = $4,471).

To continue, you must follow the online instructions. More than likely, you will click on the tab, "Trade."

Next, an order entry screen will appear. Figure 5.1 provides an example of an order entry screen for the stock YYY.

Note: Your screen may look different from the one shown in Figure 5.1.

It's easy to complete the order entry screen, but it's also easy to make mistakes. So learn to use it correctly. Mistakes can cost you money.

- *Symbol:* Enter the correct stock symbol. Sometimes investors (the careless ones) enter the wrong symbol and buy the wrong stock! Fortunately, there is a preview button that allows you to catch mistakes before you submit the order.
- *Action:* Choose to buy or sell. Because we're going to buy YYY, we select Buy.
- *Quantity:* Select how many shares to buy. For this order, we enter 100 shares.
- *Order type:* You can choose limit or market order. We select Limit Order, and I'm going to tell you why below.
- *Time in force:* You can place a time limitation on any order. The default setting is "Day," which means the order is good for today only. You can also select Good 'til Canceled, which I explain below.

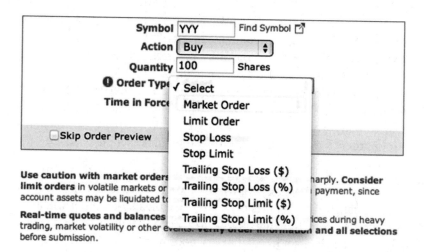

Figure 5.2

Market Order: Fast Fills at an Uncertain Price

The fastest and easiest type of order to fill is a *market order*. Let's say we look up the stock quote on YYY and see that it is trading at $44.67 to $44.71. To refresh your memory, if you wanted to buy YYY, the current ask price is $44.71, which is the most you should expect to pay if you enter the order right now. You don't like that price? Don't worry—it will change in a second. (It's kind of like the weather.)

When you place a market order, it is filled fast. Why? Because the computer grabs the lowest (published) ask price and snares the shares at that price. That is a good price for the seller, but probably not for you, the buyer. It's kind of like buying a car and paying the list price, but with no negotiations. If you want the stock quickly, you may have to pay the market price. Just remember that you are paying a little bit more because of the speed.

Example: Let's say that you place a market order to buy YYY at the current ask price. If you select, Market Order, the order is filled immediately. In our example, you bought the stock at $44.71.

The brokerage firm automatically transfers $4,471 ($44.71 × 100 shares = $4,471) plus a $10 commission out of your cash account. If you pressed the enter key, placed the order, and received confirmation of the trade, then you are now a YYY shareholder.

If YYY goes up a point, you have a paper gain (real, but not yet realized) of $100 (1 point profit × 100 shares). Although it sounds easy to watch your money work for you while you're at the beach, it's a lot harder to make and keep profits than most people realize.

Bottom line: Remember that the stock market is an auction, and you do not have to pay whatever is asked of you. Nevertheless, if you don't want to haggle over pennies per share, then the market order will meet your needs. Unfortunately, in a fast market, or with a volatile stock, market orders can get filled at a very poor price.

Fortunately, there is an alternative: the *limit order*.

Limit Order: Slower Fills at a More Competitive Price

The limit order usually takes a little more time before it is filled, but also allows you to negotiate for a better price. The advantage of a limit order is that you decide the price at which you want to buy or sell the stock. However, there is the possibility that no one will want to trade with your order, and you might not make the trade. A limit order can take a few extra seconds or minutes to fill, but don't let that deter you. Must you really buy the stock right now?

Here's how the limit order works: YYY is trading at $44.67 to $44.71 (bid-ask spread) per share and you want to buy it, but you feel you can pay less. Enter an order to buy at a limit price of $44.50. If YYY falls to $44.50 (unlikely for today), then the order will be filled at that price. If the stock never makes it to $44.50, then your order won't be filled.

Sometimes, for whatever reason, no matter where you put your limit order, you never seem to get it filled at the most competitive price. The limit order gives you a lot more flexibility. Many investors like the limit order because it puts you in control of your order.

The limit order is usually a good choice. In our example, the market is $44.67 to $44.71. If you bid $44.69, you are now the highest published bidder. No stock is allowed to trade on that exchange at a lower price—until after your bid has been filled. In other words, your limit order can be neither ignored nor hidden. All you need for your order to be filled is for a seller to enter the picture. You are doing that seller a favor by giving him or her an opportunity to trade above the specialist's bid of $44.67. Therefore, both you and the seller save $0.02 per share.

It doesn't always happen, but when the stock is trading actively, and when there are both buyers and sellers participating, there is an excellent chance your order will be filled. The downside: If the stock rallies, your bid may become too low to remain competitive, and that means the order will go unfilled.

Time: Good 'til Cancelled and Good for the Day Only

If you select a limit order, you also have choices concerning how long the order is good. For example, let's say that you place a limit order to buy 100 shares of YYY at $44.50 per share (even though the current ask price is $44.71 per share). When placing the order, you must specify whether the order is only in effect for the day (*day order*) or good until you cancel the order (*good-'til-canceled* order, or *GTC*).

If you select good 'til canceled, you don't have to worry about reentering the order every day (but be careful not to forget that the order exists). With a day order, if the brokerage doesn't fill your order that day, the order is canceled.

Example: We enter an order to buy YYY (which is trading $44.67 to $44.71) at a limit price of $44.70. We don't consider bidding less because we really want to buy the stock. So we place a limit order to buy YYY for $44.70 good for the day only.

After we place the order at the current bid price, YYY may rally to $44.75, so our order isn't filled, at least not yet. But a few minutes later, if the stock begins trading at $44.70, it is still possible that our order is not filled because there were other investors who were lined up ahead of us (and bidding $44.70). However, if enough shares trade, or if we were the earliest bidder at that price, then we will be filled. Congratulations! You just bought YYY at your price, $44.70. By using a limit order, you saved one penny in this example.

Which Is Better? Limit or Market Order

If you are new to the stock market, you probably want to know which is better—a limit or a market order. Although market orders are fast, speed is not important when it's a long-term investment (although traders may want a faster fill). For many investors, it's much more important to get the best price. With limit orders, you have an opportunity to buy or sell at a competitive price.

In my opinion, limit orders are better because they give you more control over your order. If you want to buy and have the order filled quickly, simply enter the current ask price as your limit.

Note: The only time you would use a market order is if you had to buy the stock immediately, with no time to negotiate.

Before You Press the Enter Key . . .

Even though you know how to complete the order entry screen, I strongly suggest that you do not place a trade yet. First read this book and learn about the strategies and tools that you need to be a successful investor.

Second, start small because preventing large losses is more important than earning big profits. Now is the time to learn. You can invest more money after you prove that you know what you are doing.

If you are a beginner, you will make mistakes. Everyone does. By starting with a reasonable amount of money, you will gain a great education at a low cost. Here's something you may not know: You learn the most when you lose money.

Actually, you should expect to lose money when you first enter the stock market (unless you have beginner's luck). I offer good guidance and important lessons, but experience counts. By practicing with $500 to maybe $2,000 (depending on the size of your bankroll), you will learn important lessons.

Important: Whenever you enter information on the order entry screen, double-check the order. Make sure that you entered the correct stock symbol (be sure to verify the stock name), number of shares, and order type.

Order Routing: Where Your Order Goes

After you press the enter key, here is how your order is routed behind the scenes. If you chose to buy a stock that trades on the NYSE, the order is routed to a *specialist* on the exchange, who fills your order electronically or holds it until it can be filled. If you buy a Nasdaq-listed stock, a *market maker* handles the order electronically.

As an investor, you care only that your order is executed quickly and for a reasonable price. Your online broker has software that finds the most competitive prices. The best brokers are efficient under all market conditions.

Premarket and After-Hours Trading

The regular stock market hours are 9:30 a.m. to 4:00 p.m. ET Monday through Friday. Typically, you place orders during market hours. In addition, you can trade stocks in the premarket (from 7:00 a.m. to 9:30 a.m. ET), and from 4:00 p.m. to 8:00 p.m. ET.

After-hours trading works like this: The major stock exchanges remain open for electronic trading through electronic communication networks (ECNs). In the regular market, a few billion shares are traded during the day, but only thousands are traded in the after-hours market. In fact, the volume is so small, and the bid-ask quotes are so wide that I suggest you avoid night trading altogether.

. . . .

The low volume, and especially the low liquidity, can cause strange things to happen to stock prices. If you are unfamiliar with after-hours trading, here is an unbreakable rule: Never enter a market order after hours. If you do, you can end up buying or selling a stock for a terrible price. Trading after hours is a tricky business, and my advice is to do your investing and trading during the regular hours.

Note: It's also recommended that you try to avoid the first 15 minutes after the market opens before placing a trade. The reason is that in the first 15 minutes, professional traders and institutional investors place orders, which increases the volatility. It can be a rough environment for beginners (but often profitable for experienced traders).

Bottom line: If you are new to the stock market, avoid placing orders when markets are closed.

And, now, let's take a look at selling strategies. It's easy to sell a stock, but choosing the right time to sell is a challenge.

Have a Selling Strategy

After you've placed your first order, it is now time to think about selling. It's easy to sell a stock (I'll show you how later). The hard part is selling at the right price. No matter when you sell, you always feel that you could have done better. If you sell a stock too soon, you might kick yourself for losing out on potential profits. And if you sell a stock too late, you might turn a winning position into a losing position (that is painful to your ego and your account). Your goal is to find a good price for you.

It's not easy to manage a stock position, but it's extremely important to learn how. Too many investors think of the stocks they want to buy without thinking of when to sell. Knowing when to sell is just as important as knowing when to buy, as many investors painfully discover. Buying and holding a stock forever is not a selling plan (although some investors disagree). Playing it by ear is also not a plan. So as soon you buy your first stock, think of why you may sell (and if you are truly a long-term investor, it could be years). This is having a selling strategy.

Your Selling Strategy

Your selling strategy should be customized for you and your personality and investment style. Before you buy a stock, you should know the price you want to buy at and, if you plan to be a short-term trader, a target selling price. Long-term investors cannot make a reasonable guess that goes several years in the future. Right now, you may not have an idea, and that's okay. With more experience (and after reading this book), you will learn.

By having a plan (and remaining faithful to that plan), you won't be swayed by other people's opinions (which are frequently wrong), the media, or your own emotions.

Why Sell a Stock?

Many beginners don't know that selling is a difficult part of investing. When you sell a stock for a loss, you are admitting that you made a mistake. Most investors don't like to admit their mistakes. In fact, as you gain experience, you must understand that accepting losses is an important part of being an investor. Disciplined investors and traders learn when an investment is not working and when it no longer deserves a place in their portfolio. It's better to take a small loss now rather than a much bigger loss later.

There are many reasons why you'd sell a stock. Perhaps you made so much money on the stock that you are giving "high fives" to your friends and family (always a bad sign). If that happens to you, sell soon because you may have too much money invested in that one stock.

You also sell winning positions when they are no longer performing as you expected (this takes some experience to identify). Perhaps earnings growth slowed, or the stock price might have dropped below its moving averages, which you'll learn about in Chapter 13.

One of the worst mistakes that beginners make is holding onto losing stocks for too long. In fact, most people sell their winners too soon and hold onto their losers, hoping the losers will come back to even. This is a serious mistake. As I mention throughout the book, if you own a stock that is losing money (more than 5 percent), be willing to sell. Establish a maximum loss for each stock owned, perhaps 7 or 8 percent, and sell if the losses reach that level.

Note: Not everyone agrees that you should sell losing stocks. In fact, some people believe that you should buy *more* of a stock whose price is declining (remember, that strategy is called dollar cost averaging, or buying at lower and lower prices to reduce the cost of the average share owned). Although dollar cost averaging can make sense if you are a long-term investor and are buying mutual funds, when buying individual stocks, buying more shares of a weak stock is usually a mistake.

It's very easy to lose big money by refusing to take a small loss now, hoping the stock will make a miraculous turnaround. Why chase after a stock when it is obvious you were wrong in your initial analysis? There are many other stocks with better prospects.

This is so important that I'm going to give you two rules. No matter what else you learn in this book, if you can remember these two rules, you will save yourself a small fortune over time.

- *Rule 1:* If you own a stock that has lost more than 5 percent, mark it as a warning. If that stock has lost 7 or 8 percent, sell it and find another stock to buy.
- *Rule 2:* Do not buy more shares of an individual stock that is falling in price.

> *Hint:* Do you want to know the secret to making money in the stock market or with any investment? *Don't lose money.* (Don't laugh—it's true.) Even better, don't lose too much money on any single trade. You can keep losses to a minimum if you follow the two rules above, and if you do, one day you will be thankful that you listened.

Suggestion: Print these two rules and place them in front of your computer and never forget them. On a personal note, I wish I had followed my own advice when I was a beginner. Like so many others, I thought I was smarter than the market. Big mistake!

When to Sell a Losing Stock

As I mention above, if a stock is not performing and you have lost a certain amount of money on it, perhaps 7 or 8 percent or more, sell.

Why hold onto a loser that may never get back to even? It's better to focus your time on stocks that are winning.

Another important rule about selling is this: If you have a winning stock and believe that the stock is still a good value, let it continue going higher. As I said before, and it's worth repeating: Most beginners do the opposite. They hold onto their losing stocks, hoping they'll come back to even, and sell their winners too early. A lot depends on the stock, however. For example, you will need to give volatile stocks more room than a stodgy bank stock.

Bottom line: Spend as much time thinking about selling as you do about buying. To avoid the psychological turmoil that many investors feel before selling, you should create rules for selling. The rules stated above should get you started.

Managing a Winning Stock

When holding winning stocks, investors often make two mistakes. First, they often sell the stock as soon as the trade becomes slightly profitable. And then, after selling, they miss out on the major move as the stock zooms higher.

Second, investors want to hold certain stocks forever despite the fact that some winners become losers. In fact, there is nothing worse for your ego (and account) than to watch a profit disappear and turn into a loss. There are a number of strategies to prevent this from happening.

If you are an investor, you will be thinking long term and won't worry too much about the day-to-day fluctuations in the price of your stock. Nevertheless, you should have an idea of a potential selling price. Perhaps a profit target has been reached or perhaps the stock seems overvalued based on fundamental or technical analysis (which you will learn later).

As I've said before, if a stock falls by 5 percent from its high, then put it on alert. If it moves up, that's great. If not, as soon as it falls by more than 5 percent, consider selling. If it drops by more, then sell. This will lock in your remaining profit (if any).

If you still believe that the stock is going to move higher (and don't want to sell a profitable position), then you can sell half.

It's true that you should let your winners run, but if that winner starts to move in the wrong direction, it might be time to close the position.

> *Hint:* Beginning in Part Four, you will learn about fundamental and technical analysis. Using these tools will help you determine when to sell. For example, if a company announces that its earnings are worse than expected (fundamental analysis), that could be a strong sell signal. In addition, if a stock drops below its moving average (technical analysis), that could be a sell signal. I discuss this in more detail later.

Sell Gradually

You don't have to sell all your stock at one time. In fact, you can sell gradually, maybe 10 to 20 percent of your holdings. There is no right answer because it really depends on you.

For example, if you sell all your shares of a winning stock and after you sell, the stock zooms higher, you will feel terrible. To solve this dilemma, you could have sold half the shares. This way you lock in some of the profits while giving the other half a chance to keep going up. If you have a losing stock, once you decide to sell, it's usually best to sell all the shares at one time. In other words, sell winning stocks gradually; sell losing stocks at one time.

· ·

Truthfully, it takes experience, and trial and error, to know when to let a stock run and when to take money off the table. It also takes discipline to know the difference. Every stock is different, and every stockholder is different.

> *My opinion:* As you gain experience, you will find what works for you. As for me, selling my winning stocks gradually (scaling out of a position) makes sense. There is nothing wrong with selling some of your position to lock in gains. If I'm uncomfortable with the stock and am not pleased with how it is performing, however, I might sell all shares at once, especially if the price is falling.

Hint: If you have a profitable stock that continues to rise in price, you can *add* to the position, as long as the stock is a good value. This idea appears to go against human nature and is the opposite of dollar cost averaging. Typically, you want to buy at the lowest price and sell at the highest. But often leading stocks that rally continue to go higher. Conversely, weak stocks that decline often keep going down. Trying to buy a stock as it's falling is like trying to catch a falling knife. Buying on the way up, although not for everyone, will increase profits on those powerful stocks that are rising. Those are the stocks you want to own.

Now, I'll show you ways to limit losses.

Learn How to Limit Losses

It's true that not everyone believes in selling stocks, especially buy-and-hold investors. Unfortunately, one of the most common ways to lose money is by not getting out of a stock in time. Speaking from experience, failure to cut losses on a losing stock is a sure way to lose a fortune—and your self-confidence.

As you have learned, before you buy a stock, you should have a written plan with two prices.

1. Your buy price.
2. Your planned selling price.

Finally, the plan includes a third price, an emergency escape price that limits losses. Typically, the escape price is 5 percent or more below your entry price. *Note:* Some people will use a 7 or 8 percent escape price, but you can establish your own loss limit. *Note:* Later, you will learn how to look at a chart to determine when to buy or sell.

Although it's wonderful to think of how your money can grow over the years (thanks to compounded earnings), remember that stocks do not always move higher. It's also difficult to know which ones will succeed. Therefore, always think of a price for your exit if you are wrong about the stock price. Even stocks of the best companies rise and fall over the years, especially in a correction or bear market.

Most people should have a written trading plan that includes what action to take when the trade does not go as they hoped. You don't want to "play it by ear" or assume only the best-case scenarios. Do not allow yourself to become too optimistic about the stock because you could be exposing yourself to significant risk.

After buying a stock, investors may feel hopeful and perhaps euphoric, especially when the stock price moves higher. Although you hope your stock goes up forever, it's possible that you picked a loser. Unless you are a very talented stock picker, you will have many losers. Perhaps more losers than winners. Why hold a stock that is going down? Yes, it might come back one day, but doesn't it make sense to invest in companies whose stock is going up, not down? The answer: It makes good sense.

Note: If you forced me to tell you one rule that will prevent you from losing money, first on my list would be, "Cut your losses." Many investors who buy stocks are shocked when their stock goes down. Rather than cutting their losses at a certain point (5 to 8 percent), they often hope the stock will come back to even, and they even buy more (dollar cost averaging). More often than not, it doesn't get back to even.

Therefore, to survive, it's essential that you create an escape price and stick to it, unless something dramatic occurs to change your outlook. Don't let a small loss turn into a huge loss. Get out of a losing stock when it is down more than 5 percent and doesn't appear to be coming back. Then use that money to find a stock with better prospects.

Some people can't admit they are wrong and continue to hold as their stocks fall. That 5 or 6 percent loss becomes a 10 percent loss, which turns into a 30 percent loss. Although stocks do make dramatic turnarounds, it's also possible that you'll be waiting months or years. Don't tie up your money with a losing stock when there are so many better stocks to choose from.

How to Cut Losses and Protect Gains

Cutting losses and protecting gains are essential to success. Instead of simply writing it on paper, which is a *mental stop loss*, you can enter a "hard" *stop loss* price. We discuss both methods now.

The Mental Stop Loss

Let's say that you just bought a stock for $25 per share. In your mind, you can create a "mental" stop loss. For example, you promise yourself that if the stock drops to $23 per share (an 8 percent loss), you will sell it.

Unfortunately, most investors do not have the discipline to sell a losing stock when it hits the target price. They freeze in fear when their beloved stocks fall, or they convince themselves that the lower price is only temporary. Others won't get rid of a losing stock because, "It's too cheap to sell." Perhaps they refuse to accept any loss.

The mental stop loss is more like a wait-and-see attitude. It gives the stock some room to move, but it takes a lot of discipline to sell a stock based on a mental price target. Most people probably won't sell even if the mental price is hit.

Stop-Loss Order: Protecting You from Disaster

Instead of a mental stop loss, you can use a "hard" stop loss to protect your stock portfolio. As the name implies, the purpose of a *stop-loss order* is to protect your profits (if the stock is a winner) or to cut losses (if the stock is a loser). A stop-loss order is activated once the stock trades at the stop-loss price (or lower). Stop-loss orders may be limit or market orders. First, we discuss the stop-loss *market* order.

Here's how the stop-loss market order works: You enter one price, either below your entry price to prevent a loss or below the current market price to lock in a gain. When the specified target price is hit, you've automatically created an active order. The main advantage of a stop loss is that it automates the selling process and leaves your emotions out of it. It is also useful when you are unable to watch the market.

Here's an example: Let's say that you buy XYZ at $30 per share. At the time you buy the stock, you place a stop-loss order at $28.50 per share (a 5 percent loss). This means that if XYZ trades at $28.50 or less per share, a sell order will be generated instantly. If it is a market order, the stock will be sold at the best available bid price (as with any market order). It may be sold at $28.50, but this is not guaranteed.

Figure 7.1 provides an example of a stop-loss entry screen. We are telling the computer to sell XYZ at the market after it hits $28.50 per share.

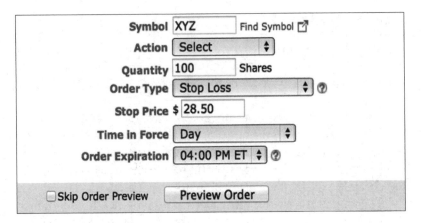

Figure 7.1   Stop loss (market)

Source: Fidelity Investments. © 2002 FMR LLC. All rights reserved. Used by permission.

Problems with the Stop-Loss Order

The stop-loss order isn't perfect. First, although it is guaranteed that your stock will be sold (if you use a market order), there are no guarantees that it will be sold at an acceptable price. In fact, one of the risks of using a stop-loss market order is that you could sell at a terrible price. Also, in volatile markets, your stop-loss order can be triggered by an unforeseen event, and you could sell at a price that is much lower than anticipated.

Here's what could happen: Let's say that you initiate a stop loss at $28.50 per share (using XYZ as an example, which is trading at $30 per share). A few days later, XYZ drops from $30 per share and is falling fast. When XYZ hits $28.50 per share, the stop loss is triggered. But because XYZ is dropping so fast, the next available price could be unexpected, such as $22.50.

In this example, the stop-loss market order was triggered at $28.50, but before the order was filled, the price declined to $22.50 per share. Instead of locking in a 5 percent loss, you just sold your stock 25 percent lower than you had intended. (It's even more annoying when XYZ, which was at $22.50 per share, suddenly rises to $30 or higher the same or the next day.)

Note: During extreme conditions, such as a "flash crash," when the market drops by hundreds of points within minutes (i.e., *gaps down*), the next available price could be much lower. (In an extreme example, during one flash crash, the next available price for many stocks was $0.01, but the exchanges canceled the trades).

Fortunately, flash crashes are infrequent, but they do expose the weakness of the stop-loss order. Fortunately, most of the time, stop-loss orders work as intended, but in a fast market, they don't.

My opinion: I personally don't like using automated (i.e., hard) stop losses because they are occasionally filled at lower-than-expected prices. In a fast market, you get a quick fill, but the price is not satisfying. The only time I'd consider a stop loss is if I were on vacation and unavailable to watch the markets. But in most cases, I'd avoid using the stop loss. You are letting the market make your selling decision.

Running the Stops

Another problem with a stop-loss order is that it is transparent. A game that some market makers played (these days, it will be computer algorithms) is "run the stops," when the stock is forced low enough to trigger a large cluster of stop-loss orders (usually at round numbers). After the stock is sold at the most popular stop-loss price, the stock reverses direction and rallies.

The biggest problem with stop losses is that you have given up control of your sell order to the computer. During volatile markets, this can cost money. Either use stop orders or don't, but give it serious consideration.

Stop-Limit Order

In many ways, the *stop-limit order* is better than the stop-loss market order. Here's how it works: Instead of entering one stop-loss number, you enter two numbers. The first number triggers the stop. The second number specifies the limit price you are willing to accept for your shares.

For example, if you have a $50 stock, you could enter a stop-limit order at $47.50 for the stop price, and $47.00 for the limit price. In this example, once the stock hits $47.50, the order is triggered. Then the sell order will be filled as long as the price is $47.00 or better. You are telling your broker's computer the minimum price you will accept.

Another example: If you have a $30 stock, you could enter a stop-limit order at $27.90 (a 7 percent stop loss) and a limit price of $27.90 (you can make the two numbers identical). In this example, once the stock hits $27.90, the order is triggered. If that $27.90 price (or better) is available, the order will be filled. If there is no longer an opportunity to sell at $27.90 or better because the stock price is falling, then your order will go unfilled.

The problem with the stop-limit order, as always, is that in a fast-moving market, the order won't get filled. This is a potential risk, which is why I suggest making the limit price a few pennies below the trigger price. On the other hand, if the market plunges and then bounces back, you'll be thankful you are using a stop-limit order rather than a stop loss. Just remember that on the rally, the (now triggered) order will get filled at your limit price. But if you really wanted to get out of the stock, the stop-limit order might *not* be what you're looking for.

Note: In my opinion, the stop-limit order is better than the stop-loss order, but it's still not ideal.

Trailing Stop Order

The trailing stop order, which is entered as a dollar or percentage amount, seems like a perfect idea. The trailing stop automatically trails behind the rising stock price and is designed to lock in gains or limit losses.

When a stock pulls back by a certain amount (a dollar amount or percentage), the order is triggered. Then it is filled, if possible. For example, if a stock rises to $50 per share, instead of manually entering a stop loss, you could enter 5 percent (see Figure 7.2) which will automatically trigger when the stock falls by 5 percent. The great thing

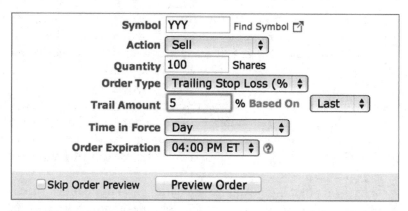

Figure 7.2   Trailing stop-loss order
Source: Fidelity Investments. © 2002 FMR LLC. All rights reserved. Used by permission.

about the trailing stop is that if the stock moves higher, the trailing stop follows along, tick by tick. Even if the stock makes a new high, it still won't trigger unless the stock pulls back by 5 percent.

The disadvantage of the trailing stop: In a fast market, the trailing stop could trigger because of a temporary market dip. But this is the chance you take when using trailing stops.

Note: It's also possible to enter a trailing stop-limit order, which can give you even more control over your order. The trailing stop market order will get you out of the stock, while the trailing stop-limit order may not get filled at all.

Note: If you want to use trailing stops, ask your brokerage firm what criteria it uses (percentages or dollar amounts), and how to enter the order.

The Best of Both Worlds: Use Price Alerts

Legendary mutual fund manager Peter Lynch once told me that stop losses were like "death by a thousand cuts." And I agree. All those losses can start to add up. But there is an alternative.

Rather than using automatic stop losses, you can set up *price alerts* for the securities you buy (and for those you plan to buy). For example, if you buy YYY at $20 per share, you can set a price alert at $19 (5 percent loss), or even at $25 (25 percent gain).

If the $19 alert is triggered, you will be notified by a sound from your computer, or perhaps you will receive an e-mail and text message. Next, you can turn to your mobile device or computer and decide what action to take. More than likely, you will sell soon depending on market conditions. And if the $25 price alert is triggered, you can sell for a profit or set new price alerts.

The main point is that you are in control of your sell orders. Technology has made price alerts practicable. Because of mobile devices, you are notified instantly if the target price is hit, allowing immediate action.

Note: Stop-loss orders still make sense if you are unable to access your account immediately, for example, if you are at work or in a meeting. In addition, if you are not disciplined and ignore price alerts, automatic stop losses might be a better alternative.

How to Sell Your Stock

Now that you know when to sell, I show you how to sell. To refresh your memory, we bought 100 shares of YYY, and since then, the stock rose by 2 points. Since we own 100 shares, we are ahead by $200.

The profits are real, but they are *unrealized* until we actually sell the stock. It's a common misperception that the profits are not real. As long as you have the opportunity to sell, those are real profits.

The mechanics of selling a stock are quite easy and can be done with a press of the button. A sample sell screen is shown in Figure 7.3.

Note: After you sell a stock, you have a two-day *settlement date*. This means that the cash is not delivered to your account until three days after the sale. However, the money is instantly available for you to buy another stock or other security because you do not have to pay for these shares until three days have passed (and the cash from the sale will be available).

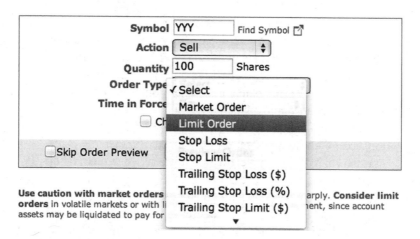

Figure 7.3   Sell order screen

Source: Fidelity Investments. © 2002 FMR LLC. All rights reserved. Used by permission.

Now that you have learned how to enter and exit a stock, it's time to learn how to make money. To be a profitable investor or trader, you need a strategy. In Part Three, I show you several winning strategies. No one strategy works perfectly in all market environments, which is why it's important to learn more than one. Then you can choose a strategy that fits your risk tolerance and time horizon (as well as current market conditions).

The Rise and Fall of Long-Term Capital Management

Investors can learn a lot from the rise and fall of Long-Term Capital Management, a hedge fund run by a group of powerful, successful and extremely intelligent academics and traders who specialized in options and other derivatives.

The Rise

In 1994, John Meriwether, a former vice chairman and head of bond trading at Salomon Brothers, founded the hedge fund Long-Term Capital Management (LTCM). Other principals of the firm included some of the best and brightest financial minds in the world, including two Nobel-prize-winning economists and a vice chairman of the Federal Reserve Board. The hedge fund began trading with more than $1 billion in investor capital.

Large investment banks and other sophisticated investors eagerly invested approximately $1.3 billion in the hedge fund, (the minimum investment was $10 million). LTCM was "destined for success," the financial media proclaimed. But there were some unusual rules. For example, because it was a hedge fund, it conducted its operations in secret. Nevertheless, for the first three years the fund had excellent although not spectacular returns.

Originally, the hedge fund created complex mathematical models that took advantage of price discrepancies between U.S., Japanese, and European government bonds. The "nondirectional" strategies it used also included profiting from merger takeovers. As its trading positions grew, LTCM took highly leveraged positions in index options such as the S&P 500, as well as stock options. At the beginning of 1998, the firm borrowed $125 billion with approximately $5 billion of equity. By any measurement, it was heavily leveraged.

The Fall

In 1998, LTCM began to unravel as its returns began to fall. It started after the Russian government devalued the ruble on its government bonds. Soon, investors began to sell Japanese and European bonds to buy U.S. Treasury bonds. This was the unanticipated event that LTCM and its computer models had not planned for. Instead of booking profits, LTCM started hemorrhaging money, creating a liquidity crisis.

By August, the hedge fund had lost $1.85 billion in capital as investors sought higher quality bonds. Up to this point, the company had been highly successful, but many of its largest investors began to sell. As rumors spread, institutional investors nervously began to pull out their money, creating a full-fledged panic. Once investors became nervous, it started a vicious cycle of additional selling.

When the money on hand decreased, LTCM managers were forced to liquidate positions to meet margin requirements at terrible prices. The more they unwound positions, the worse the prices became, and the losses increased.

Alan Greenspan, chairman of the Federal Reserve Bank of New York, arranged a multi-billion-dollar bailout for LTCM. When the accounts were cleared, the losses for LTCM totaled $4.6 billion, all within four months. Many banks simply wrote off millions of dollars in losses, while a number of top executives at various banks resigned their positions for investing so heavily in LTCM.

What Went Wrong

After the collapse of LTCM, financial experts were able to take a closer look at the mistakes made by some of the smartest people in the investment world. Critics said that the LTCM hedge fund managers didn't take into account all the possible risks.

Although LTCM had access to the most sophisticated computers and formulas, the managers didn't plan for people acting irrationally when confronted with unanticipated events, such as a devalued ruble. In addition, its highly leveraged options positions caused its positions to unravel quickly when investors pulled their money.

Ironically, according to its computer models, LTCM thought its positions were low risk. Although the hedge fund managers were extremely bright, they didn't recognize the risk of highly leveraged positions.

Note: If you'd like to learn more about the rise and fall of LTCM, you should read *When Genius Failed* (Random House), by Roger Lowenstein, which describes in detail the entire debacle. It is a good reminder that you should always plan for what could go wrong if trading stocks or options.

PART THREE

MONEY-MAKING STRATEGIES

8

Make Money Slowly: Investment Strategies Using Stocks, Mutual Funds, Index Funds, and ETFs

Before you put real money into the market, you should find an appropriate strategy. A strategy is a plan for buying and selling stocks, and is essential if you want to be a consistently profitable investor or trader. Without a strategy or plan, you will probably be switching from one idea to another with no achievable goal.

You do not want to rely on luck or tips from acquaintances to make money. That's like getting in your car in Chicago and driving in any random direction, hoping to arrive in California. If you don't prepare and plan in advance, it's likely you won't have a successful trip.

If you are new to the stock market, it's best to keep an open mind before you choose a strategy. If a particular strategy makes sense to you, take the time to study the other strategies included in this book. It can take a while before you find an investment strategy that seems right. Hopefully, it also increases the value of your portfolio.

Keep in mind that you aren't limited to one strategy. Some investors and traders use a variety of strategies, whereas others are comfortable using only one. For example, some investors expect to arrive at their destination in a day, while others plan to take a week or longer. Some investors drive faster (higher risk tolerance), while others drive at the speed limit (lower risk tolerance).

No matter what strategy you use, here are a few things to remember:

1. A strategy is only as good as the person using it. In other words, no matter how brilliant and ingenious the strategy, you must execute it well or you can still lose money.
2. Not all strategies work under all market conditions.
3. Don't become so devoted to a strategy that you are blind to the fact that you are losing money. Money is the scorecard that determines whether your strategy is working.

You have to take the time to find a strategy or strategies that fit your personality and risk tolerance. Unfortunately, there are no magic answers to finding success in the stock market. As you'll discover, many of the strategies and much of the advice you receive are contradictory. Therefore, the only way to find out what ultimately works on Wall Street is through trial and error. And now, let's get started learning about strategies.

Buy and Hold: A Popular Strategy for Investors

The idea behind the buy-and-hold strategy is that if you buy stock in a fundamentally sound company and hold it for the long term (think in terms of years), you'll realize a satisfactory return on your investment. The beauty of a buy-and-hold strategy is that you can buy a stock and watch it rise in price without constantly watching the market. The key, however, is evaluating the company to be certain it is fundamentally sound and that it is not overvalued.

Investors who bought shares of companies such as IBM and Microsoft in the early days made huge sums of money. The other advantage of buy and hold is that you're not constantly buying and selling. Buy and hold is the easiest investment strategy to use, and, during bull markets, it works wonderfully.

One of the most successful buy-and-hold investors is billionaire Warren Buffett. He rarely buys stocks in technology companies, but rather buys the stocks of mundane companies such as insurance companies and banks, and he has the skill (along with a team of independent analysts) to buy when the value is low. He also invests only in businesses that he understands.

This strategy worked for some of the world's greatest investors like Buffett and Peter Lynch, but it's not easy to find the best companies. Your job is to find several that are better than average and to know when they are no longer worth owning.

In fact, most people don't have the skills to find the right stocks, nor do they have the patience to hold for decades without selling. In the hands of a professional, buy and hold can work, although it's not perfect. When the market changes from bull to bear, buy and hold becomes a difficult path to follow as the value of your holdings steadily declines. You can lose your shirt if you don't understand why you own the stocks in your portfolio. Many people who buy and hold don't realize that they must constantly reevaluate their holdings. The strategy is not buy and forget.

For example, many investors didn't realize that technology stock prices were too high, and got smashed after the 1990s boom and bust. At the time, it seemed so easy to make money, but in reality, those still holding decades later lost most of their money. Buy and hold does work during certain market conditions, but it's not a guaranteed investment method.

Rather than buying and holding forever, another strategy is to buy and hold stocks until something fundamentally or technically changes in the company. You don't sell because of what is happening in the market, the economy, or the stock price. Rather, you focus on the business and hold your reasonably priced stocks as long as possible. This is how buy and hold should work, but it requires more work on the part of the investor. So let's call it "buy and hold when there is a good reason to hold," as opposed to buy and hope.

Hint: In Chapter 14, you will learn about the tools you need in order to determine when a stock changes from bullish to bearish.

Buy on the Dip: An Offshoot of Buy and Hold

The buy-on-the-dip strategy is another popular strategy. It works like this: When a stock you own (or want to own) goes down in price, especially if you believe the decline is only temporary because the company is still fundamentally sound, you buy shares (or more shares). The idea is that because the market tends to go up over time (or generally has in the past), the shares you bought at a lower price will eventually be worth more. People who buy low make money as the shares they bought kept going higher.

The problem with buying on the dip is that stocks sometimes dip two or three times and never recover. In the past, millions of people poured their life savings into stocks that seemed like bargains but actually were extremely overpriced. Many financial stocks that were hitting all-time lows kept going lower, even as new buyers stepped in. In worst-case scenarios, some stocks didn't just dip; they plunged.

When you buy on the dip, you're taking a chance. You hope you are buying a stock that is on sale, but you could be buying a stock that is damaged goods.

Exception: There are times when buying on the dip makes sense. First, if leading stocks are temporarily going down along with the entire market, you can buy these stocks at a bargain price. Just know that you may buy too early as stock prices continue to decline. In addition, if you are using short-term trading tactics and a leading stock suddenly plunges because the entire sector is going down, you may be able to make a quick profit if you buy on the dip and get the timing exactly right (but it's difficult). These are strategies that require experience, and they can work for certain traders.

Bottom Fishing: Finding Bargains Among Unloved Stocks

If you are a bottom fisher, you look for stocks that are so low that they seem to have hit bottom and have nowhere to go but up. If you find one of these gems, you can make a lot of money if it eventually recovers. Many stocks are unknown and unloved in their early days, and finding one of these is a rewarding experience. This strategy, however, requires patience, and is not for those with a short-term view.

The danger of bottom fishing is that you never know exactly when the bottom has been reached. For example, when a high-flying stock drops from $100 per share to $15, many people think it's a bargain and buy more shares, assuming that the stock can't go lower. (Maybe these were the same people who bought the stock at $50, $40, and $30.)

At this point, the stock is likely in a "death spiral," and the diving stock price suggests there is something very wrong, although you may not know what it is until later.

Because it could be years before many of these once-loved stocks rise in price, you have to be extremely confident that this once-great company has the ability to rise from the ashes. Unfortunately, most do not. Stocks that are in the basement tend to stay there a while. Nevertheless, I have spoken with professional bottom fishers who are willing to wait two or three years before scooping up favorite stocks that other investors have ignored. Successful pros can pick out stocks that are likely to recover and the ones that won't. It's not easy to do, which is why bottom fishing is not for the faint of heart.

Dollar Cost Averaging: A Systematic Way to Buy Stocks

Instead of buying stocks whenever you have extra money in your pocket, with *dollar cost averaging* you buy stocks on a regular, systematic basis. You invest a set amount of money, perhaps $100 every month. The positive side of a negative situation (when your stocks decline, that is negative) is that as you buy more stock, your average price per share moves lower. Remember: The idea is to keep buying more shares every month.

For example, let's say that you invest $250 in YYY when it is $20 per share. The next month YYY drops to $18, so you invest another $250 (assuming you have the discipline to keep investing after a 10 percent decline). As long as the market keeps coming back, dollar cost averaging will be a winning strategy. The problem is that some stocks keep dropping because the outlook for the company and its business is bad. That's why re-evaluating the company before each new investment is a good idea.

> *Hint:* Later in this chapter you will learn that dollar cost averaging into an index fund or mutual fund is a useful strategy.

A strategy similar to dollar cost averaging is called *averaging down.* With this strategy, instead of investing a set amount of money each period, you buy additional shares of stock that is on the way down. With dollar cost averaging, you have a plan. With averaging down, you buy additional shares of stock whenever you please.

Unfortunately, history has taught us that if you dollar cost average as individual stocks are falling, there are no guarantees you will ever make your money back. Therefore, if you follow my advice and exit after a 7 or 8 percent loss, then you will avoid strategies such as dollar cost averaging and averaging down. (That is my opinion based on years of trial and error.)

Note: One of the problems with buying on the dip, bottom fishing, and dollar cost averaging is that it's hard to know you've really hit bottom. Often, weak stocks get weaker or remain in the basement for years. Too many declining stocks are simply overpriced and not worth owning. The only time you might consider these strategies is if you buy quality stocks that are temporarily on sale.

Value Investing: Buying Good-Quality Companies at a Cheap Price

Value investors primarily use fundamental analysis (which is explained in Chapter 11) to pick good-quality stocks that are a bargain compared with their actual value. In other words, value investors look for stocks that are on sale.

Often, value investors will buy stocks in companies that other investors don't want. These are the low P/E (price/earnings ratio, explained in Chapter 12) stocks of companies whose earnings grow slowly, such as insurance companies and banks. Value investors are long-term investors and are willing to wait years for their investment in such stocks to become profitable.

Value investing works well during flat and high-growth market environments, but in a bear market, many value stocks decline along with the rest of the market. If these are truly value stocks, the decline should be slower than that of the average stock.

Many individual investors don't have the time to analyze a company's fundamentals. If you don't have the time or motivation to find stocks that are a good value, you can buy a mutual fund that invests in value stocks. This may not be as much fun as making your own investing decisions, but it's fun to make money.

Growth Investing: Buying Growing Companies at Any Price

The opposite of value investing is growth investing. Typically, *growth investors* use fundamental analysis to find stocks that are growing faster than the economy or are increasing earnings more rapidly than other stocks in the same, or competitive, industries. Growth investors like to see earnings growing by at least 15 or 20 percent a year for the next three or four years (although each growth investor has his or her own criteria). These stocks don't usually pay dividends because extra cash is plowed back into the growing company.

Growth investing works best during a bull market, when stocks are going higher and the price to earnings ratio (P/E) is expanding. Some years, growth investors can see returns of 100 percent or more, depending on the stocks. Typically, growth investors buy technology stocks whose earnings growth is expected to accelerate.

Unfortunately, all good things come to an end. Eventually companies become too large for growth to continue at such high compounded rates (15 percent or more). When growth slows, the stock will not perform as it did in the past. Then it's decision time. The growth investor should sell and find another opportunity.

Although the rewards are tremendous when investors discover a good growth stock, this is not an everyday occurrence. Even the stock prices of excellent technology companies such as Google and Apple plunge on occasion. Growth investing is an exciting strategy requiring excellent skills in determining which stocks to buy, but these volatile stocks tend to be risky investments.

Note: If you are interested in growth investing, you can also buy a mutual fund that invests in growth stocks.

Momentum Investing: Buy High and Sell Higher

An offshoot of growth investing is *momentum investing.* Typically, this method involves buying stocks whose prices have already exploded with the hope that momentum keeps the price rising. This has nothing to do with fundamental analysis or the future prospects of the business. This is all about trading the stock price. Momentum investors stay with the stocks as long as the momentum remains in effect. Basically, they buy higher and sell higher.

In bull markets, momentum investing works like a charm (come to think of it, almost all strategies work well in a bull market!). However, not everyone is a fan of momentum investing. Some critics call this strategy the "greater fool theory," which means that no matter how high the stock price is, you will always be able to find a bigger fool who is willing to buy it from you at a higher price. Short-term traders might use this strategy, but keep in mind that they hold only as long as there is momentum.

Momentum investing, although exciting and potentially profitable, is difficult. Although it's possible to catch some of these stocks on the upside, it is definitely not as easy as it seems. This is a strategy that requires skill and discipline. (Perhaps you should wait for the next bull market before using a momentum strategy, and if you're a beginner, you may want to skip this strategy altogether.)

Mutual Funds: A Convenient Way to Buy Stocks, Bonds, or Commodities

For many investors, *mutual funds* are an excellent idea. Instead of investing directly in the stock market, you can buy mutual funds.

An investment company creates a mutual fund by pooling investors' money and using that money to invest in an assortment of stocks, bonds, fixed income, or alternative investments such as commodities. In a way, investing in a mutual fund is like hiring your own professional money manager.

The fund manager takes pooled money from thousands of investors and uses it to buy stocks (or bonds, or whatever is allowed by the terms of the fund). The advantage is that you leave the buying and selling decisions to the fund manager (although there is an annual fee, and sometimes a load, i.e. sales commission).

There are mutual funds for every conceivable strategy or industry. For example, you could buy a mutual fund that invests in stocks (called a stock fund), technology (a sector fund), bonds (a bond fund), or one that invests in international stocks (an international fund) or in gold (commodity). No matter what kind of investment you're interested in, there is a mutual fund that should meet your needs.

Mutual funds can be the answer for people who don't have the time or knowledge to research individual companies. If you want to invest in growth or value stocks and don't have the motivation to find them on your own, you can invest in a growth or value mutual fund. This is one of the reasons that mutual funds are so popular.

Many people invest in mutual funds through 401(k) plans or IRAs, which we discuss later. You can also buy mutual funds through your brokerage firm. There are as many mutual funds as there are individual stocks.

For a fee (ranging from 0.25 percent to 8 percent for specialized funds), mutual funds give you instant *diversification.* For a minimum investment of a few hundred dollars (although some mutual funds have higher minimums), you can buy a slice of a basket of stocks.

Your brokerage firm has a list of all of the mutual funds you can buy, each with its own style and strategy. In fact, finding a quality mutual fund is almost as time consuming as finding individual stocks.

Hint: Avoid mutual funds with high management fees and loads (sales charges) because it will be exceedingly difficult for the fund to beat the major market indexes once these expenses are taken into account.

Note: If you wish, you also can invest directly in the mutual fund by writing a check or through a payroll plan that automatically takes money out of your paycheck.

Why People Choose Mutual Funds

The main reason that people choose mutual funds is they are looking for diversification. This means that instead of investing money in only one stock—a risky move—you buy a slice of hundreds of stocks. This provides diversification, which reduces the volatility in your portfolio.

For example, let's say that you bought stock in Lehman Brothers, which was one of the most successful investment banks in the United States. Unfortunately, during the housing crisis, Lehman Brothers went bankrupt. If you had owned Lehman Brothers stock, you might have lost 80 to 90 percent of your money as the stock plunged in value.

On the other hand, if you owned a mutual fund that owned Lehman Brothers stock, you might have lost no more than 3 percent of your money because of the other investments in the fund. This is the power of diversification and one reason why people like mutual funds.

However, some people want much bigger profits, which is what brings them to the stock market. If you own shares in a mutual fund that contains a stock that goes up 20 percent in one day, you might make 1 or 2 percent profit on your fund that day. But if you owned the stock directly, you would make 20 percent.

If you have never invested in the stock market, you may consider getting your feet wet with mutual funds. You should know that there are two types of funds: *no-load* and *load.* Important: You are much better off with a *no-load fund* (which means that you won't have to pay extra sales charges or hidden fees for investing in the fund) because it's less expensive. As mentioned earlier, those fees (*load fund*) make it hard for the fund to beat the market indexes.

Bottom line: If you invest in mutual funds, choose no-load funds.

The Problem with Mutual Funds

Mutual funds aren't perfect, of course. After all, mutual funds are designed to provide a diversified portfolio and to outperform the market averages. They are not designed, however, to make money at all times. Therefore, most mutual funds do well in bull markets and not so well during bear markets (although a handful of specialized long/short mutual funds are designed to limit losses in bear markets).

In addition, most mutual fund managers (over 80 percent) don't beat the index averages each year. Therefore, before buying a mutual fund, look closely at its expenses and extra fees. Some mutual funds charge less than 1 percent each year in fees, while specialized funds may have sales loads as high as 8 percent. It's extremely difficult for many mutual funds to outperform the market while saddling investors with high fees.

In addition, many mutual funds charge a redemption fee if you sell the mutual fund in less than 30 days. When you buy mutual funds, the idea is to hold them for the long term, and many funds penalize you if you sell too soon (less than 30 days).

Note: You can also view independent articles about mutual funds by reading print or online editions of *Kiplinger, Barron's, Forbes, Investor's Business Daily*, or the *Wall Street Journal*. You can also find mutual fund ratings using an Internet search engine. Type "rate top mutual funds" followed by the current year.

> *Hint:* The website Morningstar (www.morningstar.com) is an excellent resource for mutual fund information. It provides detailed information about each fund, a rating, and the fund objective. Morningstar is the first place to go if you want to learn more about mutual funds.

Note: There are hundreds of fund families but a few of the largest families with no-load funds include Fidelity, Vanguard, Pimco, T. Rowe Price, and Dodge & Cox, to name a few.

Net Asset Value

A net asset value (NAV) is similar to a stock price except that it is calculated only once per day. It is the value of one share in a mutual fund. You can find the NAV on your brokerage firm screen, online, or at Morningstar.

Calculating the cost of buying a mutual fund is simple. For example, if you want to buy 100 shares of a mutual fund with an NAV of $10, it will cost you $1,000 (100 × $10 = $1,000). Unlike with stocks, most people invest a specified number of dollars rather than buying a specific number of shares.

You can look online to see how well your mutual fund did during various periods, from yesterday to 10 years ago. Performance records are well publicized. Just remember that there is no guarantee that how a fund performed in the past will be repeated in the future. Fortunately, if you don't like a fund's investment performance, you can easily switch to another mutual fund (but you must hold long enough to avoid a redemption fee).

Index Funds: If You Can't Beat Them, Join Them

Mutual fund managers invest in stocks they believe will outperform the market, and this means beating the market indexes. These fund managers are actively involved in improving the performance of their mutual fund, which is why they're called active managers.

Index funds are run differently. Like mutual funds, they use money pooled by investors. But unlike mutual funds, index funds do not have active managers. They simply buy the stocks that are included in one of the various indexes. In other words, instead of beating the market, index funds mimic the market.

For example, you could buy funds that track the performance of the Dow 30 index, the S&P 500 index, the Nasdaq Composite index, the Russell 2000, Wilshire 5000, and more. The idea is that if you can't beat the indexes, you might as well invest directly in them for reduced management fees. Therefore, if the Dow index is having a good year and is up 10 percent, you will get a 10 percent return on your index fund.

Index funds are less expensive than mutual funds because you don't have to pay an active manager, there are no extra sales charges, and they have lower expenses (typically less than 0.50 percent).

For these reasons, index funds have become very popular. As mentioned earlier, more than 80 percent of portfolio managers fail to beat the indexes (in some years, the records are even worse). This is why index funds are an excellent alternative.

Because index funds are designed to match the market, they obviously do well during bull markets and poorly during bear markets or a correction. Nevertheless, index funds are extremely attractive because of their low cost. If you don't want to take the time to investigate mutual funds or stocks, then index funds might be what you're looking for. This is also the ideal choice for long-term investors.

> *Hint:* Although the strategy, dollar cost averaging, can be risky when buying individual stocks, it makes sense when buying mutual funds or index funds for the long term.

Note: In Chapter 10, I include an interview with John Bogle, the man who created the first index fund. He will tell you why index funds are still the best way to invest in the stock market.

Investing in Mutual Funds or Index Funds with a 401(k) or an IRA

One of the easiest ways to invest in mutual funds or index funds is through a 401(k), a voluntary tax-deferred savings plan that is provided by a number of companies. The popular 401(k) plan is one of the reasons that so many people are involved in the stock market. The brilliant part of the 401(k) is that you don't have to pay taxes on either the invested dollars or the earnings until the cash is withdrawn at age 59½ or later (talk to a tax accountant for the specific rules).

If you leave the company before you retire, you can convert your 401(k) to an IRA (individual retirement account), another type of tax-deferred savings plan. IRA rules are complex, and the rules occasionally change, so seek professional tax advice before participating or making any changes to your plan.

Bottom line: If you have the opportunity to participate in a 401(k) or an IRA, do so. Many companies match your contributions (up to a specified limit), taxes are deferred, and there are many investment choices (usually mutual funds and index funds, but individual stocks can be bought with some plans). One of the reasons you are reading this book is to help you understand the stock market. This should help you make better investment choices if you are participating in a 401(k) or IRA.

Investing in ETFs: A Clever Way to Spice Up Your Portfolio

Exchange-traded funds (ETFs) have boomed in popularity. An ETF is similar to a mutual fund but trades like a stock; that is, it can be bought or sold intraday (unlike mutual funds; which *cannot* be traded intraday). ETFs consist of a basket of securities that track a specific index or specific sectors. You buy and sell ETFs through your brokerage firm. If you think that ETFs sound like mutual funds, you are right. The main difference is that there is usually no active manager, which is why ETFs charge a very small management fee. Note: A few ETFs have active managers.

There are thousands of ETFs, and new ones are created each year. The most popular ETFs are those that track the major indexes such as the Dow Jones Industrial Average (DIA), Nasdaq-100 (QQQ), S&P 500 (SPY), and Russell 2000 (IWM).

Just like mutual funds, you can also find ETFs that track industry sectors. For example, there are semiconductor, oil service, biotechnology, retail, and pharmaceutical ETFs.

You can also buy fixed income ETFs, which include mostly bonds and Treasuries. There are international ETFs that are country-specific, for example, a Japan index fund or a Brazil index fund. Here's the benefit: If you were trading stocks and wanted to buy a specific sector, you'd have to buy multiple stocks to imitate that sector. On the other hand, you can buy one ETF that gives you diversification by tracking an entire sector.

Another advantage of trading ETFs is that most are liquid (a few are not), which means that it's easy to get into and out of them. In addition, because they consist of a basket of individual stocks, ETFs provide instant diversification. After all, it would be too costly and time consuming to own so many individual stocks in a specific sector or index.

You can create your own basket of ETFs that will suit any strategy, from short-term trading to long-term investing. Just like stocks, ETFs can be bought and sold on an exchange. And just like mutual funds, ETFs include a basket of stocks that can meet any investor's needs.

With most mutual funds, there are extra fees if you hold the fund for less than 30 days. On the other hand, you can buy, hold, or trade ETFs like a stock. If you think that ETFs sound like a good idea, they are. They are easy to buy and sell, provide instant diversification, and annual expenses are lower than those of most mutual funds.

Disadvantages of ETFs

The disadvantages of trading ETFs are similar to those of trading stocks. There are many ETFs so you have to choose carefully. Just as with stocks, it's possible to lose money if you choose the wrong ETF and if you aren't disciplined in managing risk.

> *Hint:* Choose ETFs with a lot of volume and liquidity. When it's time to sell, you want to be able to get out of the ETF quickly.

Warning: Do Not Buy Leveraged ETFs

Although there are many advantages to ETFs, there is one type of ETF that should be avoided. It is called a *leveraged* ETF, and it promises to give you two or three times the return of the underlying index. In reality, leveraged ETFs are primarily for traders who buy and sell on the same day.

Because of the way these funds change their portfolios on a daily basis and the arithmetic behind daily compounding, leveraged ETFs often do not provide the anticipated returns. Most leveraged ETFs are too risky, and over the long term, you're almost guaranteed to lose money. Unless you are a day trader, I strongly suggest avoiding leveraged ETFs.

· ·

In the next chapter, you'll learn about short-term trading strategies. Even if you have no interest in trading stocks or ETFs, it's worth your time to learn the strategies. You never know when you might need to use them.

9

Want to Make Money Fast? Short-Term Trading Strategies

If you want to take advantage of quick stock price movements, you will be interested in short-term trading strategies. These strategies are popular with aggressive traders who attempt to make money quickly by taking advantage of volatile stock prices and market conditions. These traders primarily use *technical analysis* to look for profitable trading opportunities, although a few traders also look at certain fundamental data (such as earnings) before buying or selling stocks. (In Part Four, you will learn how to use several tools to analyze stocks.)

Note: Even if you are primarily an investor, it is useful to learn short-term trading strategies. The more strategies you understand, the more of an edge you will have over other investors. There are certain market conditions in which short-term strategies are effective.

Day Trading: Buying and Selling in Minutes

Unlike investors, who may wait years before selling, *day traders* buy and sell stocks or ETFs within seconds, minutes, or hours (or in microseconds if a high-frequency trader). Using technical analysis, day traders try to anticipate when a stock has reached a very short-term bottom (or top). They want to pick up a small sum on each of their many daily trades. Day traders often use customized trading software to buy and sell stocks and ETFs and move into cash by the end of each day.

Day trading (or *intraday trading*) was so popular in the late 1990s that thousands of people quit their jobs to trade full time. As the market went up, everyone seemed to be making money. It all came to an abrupt end when a bear market hit, wiping out the accounts of most day traders. So many people lost money that the SEC changed the rules.

Now, you must have a minimum of $25,000 in a margin account if you make more than four intraday trades within five business days. For example, if you buy YYY Manufacturing on Monday and sell the stock before the end of the day, that is considered a day trade. If you buy YYY on Tuesday and sell on Wednesday, that is not a day trade. As a result of this rule change, smaller investors were no longer able to use the day trading strategy.

It's also a challenging strategy. Even with the best equipment and software, only a small percentage of people consistently make money day trading. First, it takes an incredible amount of discipline and knowledge to be a successful day trader. Although day traders can make money, it is an extremely difficult way to make a living.

Although day trading is not for everyone, it is a strategy that works during certain market conditions, usually when the market is volatile. This is when you would be glad that you know how to day trade. As long as you don't make more than four intraday trades within that five-day period (on accounts with less than $25,000), you can use the strategy.

Note: If you want to learn day trading strategies, you can start by reading my book *Start Day Trading Now* (Adams Media). In addition to day trading, I discuss other short-term trading strategies where you hold for a few days or a week rather than only a day. Another strategy is to find a stock that is a good candidate for day trading, and trade only that one stock. Basically, you attempt to become an expert on that stock.

Other Short-Term Trading Strategies

In addition to day trading, there are other short-term strategies, which are discussed below.

Swing Trading

When you buy a stock and sell it several days later, you are *swing trading*. The idea is to sell when the stock price reaches a predetermined target. During certain market conditions, this strategy can be successful. Basically, you buy at technical support levels and sell when your profit target is hit.

Personal note: During bull markets, I used to swing trade the strong, leading stocks in sectors such as biomedical or technology. I'd buy during the week and sell a day or two later after a strong rally. If there were no rally, I'd sell by the end of the week since there was no reason to hold.

Often, I traded only one stock (only the strongest one) but learned everything about its personality (i.e., how high or low its price went each day). Sometimes, I'd buy the stock for a longer-term hold (my core account) and buy additional shares for swing trading (my short-term account). With the power of a bull market behind me, the strategy often worked.

Position Trading

For long-term traders, there is a strategy called *position trading*. You buy a stock and hold it for a few weeks or months. This is another strategy that works well during bull markets. Unlike buy-and-hold investors, position traders will not hold indefinitely, and they will sell a position when profit targets are reached.

Note: Once again, position trading works extremely well during certain market conditions. The idea of position trading is not to buy and hold forever, but to sell when the market trend ends or when you earn the profits you anticipated. If you use this strategy, you want to choose the strongest stocks in the strongest sectors. (There are also short-term strategies you can use in a bear market, which I discuss later in this chapter.)

Although buy-and-hold investing requires fewer decisions and less work, swing trading and position trading can be rewarding. On the other hand, short-term trading strategies are more difficult because you have to study the market, learn how to use technical analysis, and keep your emotions under control. For these reasons, it's hard for many people to use short-term strategies.

Trend Trading

Typically, traders want to buy stocks that are following a bullish market trend. There are actually three types of trends: *uptrend, downtrend,* and *sideways trend.* Therefore, if a stock is moving higher and higher, it is in an *uptrend.* When the trend ends, the idea is to sell. Identifying stocks that are in an uptrend is not as easy as it seems, but it is a strategy that does work.

In fact, following the market trend can be very effective. If the overall market is bullish or your stock is in an uptrend (it's going up), then you buy and hold or use short-term bullish strategies. If the market trend turns bearish or your stock is in a *downtrend,* you will sell the stock (or sell short). On paper, following the trend seems simple. In real life, it's not always evident whether it's a bull or a bear market.

Note: Most experienced traders use more than one strategy depending on market conditions. In fact, one of the characteristics of good traders is flexibility. Trading is not for everyone mainly because of the emotional demands.

My opinion: I believe that every investor should become familiar with short-term trading strategies. Although no one expects you to be a full-time trader, using the tools and strategies of a short-term trader can work, although it requires more decisions than buy and hold.

Nevertheless, I don't want you to believe that short-term trading is easy, because it's not. Remember: More than 80 percent of professional fund managers can't beat the market averages using a variety of strategies. So how do you get started? At first, your main goal is to learn as much as you can about the market. You want to improve as a trader rather than trying to make a fortune. As you gain experience, knowledge, and discipline, you attempt to keep mistakes to a minimum while increasing profits.

For now, let's take a look at a fascinating but challenging short-term strategy: *selling short*. Instead of making a profit when the market goes up, you profit when the market goes down. Even if you will never sell a stock short, it is important to know how it's done.

Selling Short: Profiting from a Falling Stock

When you invest in a stock hoping that it will rise in price, you are said to be *long* the stock. Your goal is to buy low and sell high (or buy high and sell higher). Your profit is the difference between the buy price and the sale price.

On the other hand, if you own a position that profits when a stock goes *down* in price, you are said to be *short* the stock. When you short a stock, you first sell the stock, hoping to buy it back at a lower price. Your profit is the difference between the buy and the sale. In other words, it is the same as buying except in reverse. If you've never shorted stocks, it sounds strange until you do it a few times.

Imagine making money when a stock goes down in price. For many people, it sounds unethical to profit from a falling stock. In reality, you're in the market for only one reason—to make money. It doesn't matter whether you go long or short as long as you make profits. It's neither unethical nor inappropriate to short stocks. It's a sophisticated strategy that allows you to profit even during dismal economic conditions.

For example, let's say that you are watching the stock of YYY Company, and you believe that over the next month it will go down in price. Perhaps there is negative news about the industry, or perhaps you notice that the company has a lot of debt. You decide to short 100 shares of YYY at the current market price of $20 per share.

You can either call your brokerage firm or use your online account. When your order is filled and the stock has been sold, the brokerage firm will lend you 100 shares of YYY.

In this example, the 100 shares of stock are worth $2,000 ($20 × 100). Let's say YYY falls to $18 per share and is now worth $1,800 ($18 × 100). You can buy the shares at $18, return the borrowed shares, and lock in a two-point profit, or $200. Note: You probably have to pay margin interest on the funds that you borrowed.

Although selling short sounds like a straightforward strategy, a lot of things can go wrong. First, when you go long a stock, the most you can lose is everything you invested. (I know, that's pretty bad.) On the other hand, when you short a stock, you can lose *more* than you invested, which is why shorting is risky, especially if you are not disciplined.

Here's another example: Let's say you are wrong and YYY goes higher. For every point YYY goes up, you lose $100. How high can YYY rise? The answer is frightening: An infinite amount!

The problem with shorting is that if the stock goes up, your losses are incalculable. Keep in mind that most experienced short sellers are disciplined enough to cover (i.e., close) their short position when a stock goes against them. *Note:* If you do short, it's essential that you limit potential losses to 7 or 8 percent using stop losses.

I know people who shorted 100 shares of a gold ETF (the ticker symbol is GLD), thinking it could never go higher. They were convinced that this ETF was overpriced at $100 per share. Maybe they were right, but gold continued to go up. They eventually lost $8,000 as the gold ETF climbed from $100 to over $180. That hurts.

Obviously, when the pain got too great, they covered their positions (i.e., they bought back the ETF at a much higher price), and they had huge losses. Eventually, GLD did drop back down, but it was too late for my acquaintances because they had already closed the position.

> *Hint:* If you strongly believe that the market (rather than an individual stock) is going down, I believe you are better off buying an inverse ETF fund (discussed next). Although most investors prefer going long than short, shorting is a strategy that is important to understand.

Also, it's useful to listen to short sellers. Too often, investors delude themselves into thinking that the market, or their stock, will always go higher. Professional short sellers are good at poking holes in the "too-good-to-be-true" proclamations of market bulls. In my opinion, you should listen to both sides of an argument, but in the end, you should do what you think makes the most sense, and based on evidence, not opinion.

Selling Short Using ETFs

In the previous chapter, I explained how to invest in ETFs. Another advantage of ETFs is that you can use them to short the market. For example, if you are bearish about the market, you can buy *inverse* ETFs, which include a basket of securities that have been *sold short*. In other words, if the market goes down, the inverse ETFs go up.

One idea is to buy a non-leveraged *inverse* fund that is designed to track the S&P 500 index, but in the opposite direction. The advantage is that instead of having to learn how to short an individual stock, you let the ETF do the shorting for you. If you believe an index is going to drop in price, an inverse ETF can make sense. Because the ETF is diversified, it is less risky than shorting an individual stock (as long as it's not a leveraged ETF).

For example, let's say that you believe the S&P 500 is going to plunge. First, you should have valid fundamental or technical reasons for coming to this conclusion. Receiving a tip from a friend or reading a scary article warning of a crash is not a valid reason to short the market. Nevertheless, if you are convinced that the market will plunge, you could sell short every stock in the index, which would be extremely costly, especially if you're wrong. Rather than selling short stocks in the index, you could also buy an inverse non-leveraged ETF.

Let's say you buy 100 shares of RWM, which is an inverse of the Russell 2000 index. If the Russell 2000 falls in price, then RWM will go up (almost on a 1-to-1 percentage move correlation). For example, if the Russell 2000 goes down by 1 percent, RWM will go up by approximately 1 percent. Conversely, if the Russell 2000 goes up by 2 percent, RWM will go down by approximately 2 percent. You can also buy the inverse of the S&P 500 index (NYSE: SH), an inverse of the Dow Jones index (NYSE:DOG), or an inverse of the Nasdaq-100 index (NYSE:PSQ).

Buyer Beware: Trading Penny Stocks

Penny stocks are stocks that usually sell for less than $3 per share (although some people define a penny stock as one selling for less than $5 per share). Because the stocks of these small corporations usually don't meet the minimum requirements for listing on a major stock exchange, they trade in the over-the-counter market (OTC) on the Nasdaq. They are also called *pink sheet* stocks because at one time the names and prices of these stocks were printed on pink paper.

Many investors trade penny stocks because the share price is low and they can afford to buy many shares. For example, with only $1,000 you can buy 2,000 shares of a penny stock at $0.50. If the stock ever makes it to a dollar, you made a 100 percent profit. That is the false beauty of penny stocks, and in fact, the low price is often an illusion.

For example, you could buy a penny stock for $1.00 and watch it drop to $0.60 a couple of days later. It happens all the time with these stocks. After all, penny stocks are cheap for a reason. That reason could be poor management, no earnings, or too much debt, but whatever it is, there usually aren't enough buyers to make the stock go higher. Even with their low price, the trading *volume* on penny stocks is exceptionally low. For example, a stock like Apple will trade millions of shares per day, whereas a penny stock might trade 10,000 shares, or sometimes even less.

A number of traders specialize in these stocks, although doing so requires a different mindset. *One problem:* With a low-volume penny stock, it's easy for someone to manipulate the price. Manipulation? Yes, it happens, especially with "the pennies." If you have a $1 stock that is trading only 25,000 shares a day, when someone comes in to buy 10,000 shares, that trade is likely to affect the price. (That's also why some people with big bucks *prefer* to trade penny stocks.)

Because of their low volume, penny stocks are also the favorite investment of unethical people who try to convince you to buy a nearly worthless stock. They might call you on the phone, send e-mails, or post positive press releases they created in online websites.

A bit of advice: If a cold-calling salesperson or stranger begs you to buy a penny stock, don't listen. You might hear this: "Hey, buddy, the stock is only $0.10 per share. For $1,000, you can buy 10,000 shares. If the stock goes to a dollar, you could make $10,000. How does that sound? So can I count on you for 10,000 shares? Trust me, this stock is hot."

Thousands of people fall for this scam every day, and often by e-mail. The penny stockbrokers are skilled at making you feel that you are going to miss out on the deal of a lifetime if you don't buy in the next

10 minutes. In reality, it's unlikely that the penny stock will ever claw its way out of the basement. And if it's really that good, why are they calling you? (An entertaining movie called *Boiler Room* described some of the tactics used to convince unsuspecting investors to buy penny stocks.) If you're a beginner, my advice is not to trade penny stocks.

If You Must Trade Penny Stocks

After all these warnings, if you insist on trading penny stocks, here are a few guidelines. First, ignore the hype that you read in e-mails or on social media. They are almost guaranteed to contain bogus information. In addition, many of the penny stock newsletters are paid for by the company to pump up the price of the stock.

If you are going to invest in penny stocks, choose the ones with good earnings that have made 52-week highs. And if you do make a 30 percent profit, for example, sell quickly. That 30 percent gain could quickly evaporate. Focus only on penny stocks with a lot of volume, at least 100,000 shares a day. Stocks with less volume don't have enough liquidity and are easily manipulated.

Also, never use hard market stop-loss market orders with penny stocks as you can get filled at terrible prices. Use mental stops or price alerts. If you do get lucky (or you gain a lot of experience), do not be greedy. Try to use a small amount of money to make bigger money. Penny stocks have a bad reputation for a reason, and they are cheap for a reason, so beware.

If you are curious and want to view the prices of unlisted over-the-counter stocks, visit the website www.otcbb.com. Before investing in one of these stocks, read the warning below.

Warning: Pump and Dump Schemes

If you buy stocks because of a tip you received (and we're all guilty when we're rookies), then you could be a victim of a "pump and dump." First, company insiders in small over-the-counter companies (i.e., penny stocks) try to convince thousands of people that investing in their company is a "once-in-a-lifetime" opportunity.

The fraudsters pump up interest in the stock by posting positive messages in chat rooms, going on television or radio, and posting overly optimistic press releases. Occasionally, you may get a phone call from a broker. The idea is to artificially pump up the price of a stock by spreading false news to people who then buy shares. The stock price rises because of increased buying and speculation, not because of increased earnings.

As the stock goes higher, those with inside knowledge are prepared for the "dump." As more people buy shares of the stock, the insiders sell all their shares for a huge profit. Eventually, the truth comes out, and the stock price falls as more people sell. Guess who is left holding the shares of the now nearly worthless stock? You guessed it—the unsuspecting investors who bought into the hype. They probably thought the price could go higher, so they never sold their shares.

The pump and dump is one of the oldest and most effective scams. Usually, pump and dumps are used on penny stocks selling for less than a dollar per share because such stocks are easier to manipulate.

. . . .

Now that you have read about some of the strategies that are not recommended, I want to introduce you to two strategies that work. If you are a beginner, pay close attention as I introduce you to two legendary investors, William O'Neil and John Bogle. Their strategies are different, but their results are the same. You can use their strategies to make money.

If you are first starting out, you can't go wrong following their advice.

Legendary Investors William O'Neil and John Bogle

Wall Street Legend William J. O'Neil

Before we discuss William O'Neil, let's discuss a successful investment system he developed.

Introducing CAN SLIM

If you're a beginner, you need a disciplined method of picking stocks, and one of the best is CAN SLIM, a rule-based investing system that combines both technical and fundamental analysis. William J. O'Neil, founder and publisher of *Investor's Business Daily*, developed the CAN SLIM Investment System, which includes a number of important rules that have kept millions of investors on the right side of the market.

Each letter in CAN SLIM stands for a performance characteristic that historically winning stocks have had before they launched their big price climbs. Ideally, a winning stock should have all these attributes, according to O'Neil's writings in his best-selling book

How to Make Money in Stocks (McGraw-Hill). Here are the seven performance characteristics in CAN SLIM:

C: Current quarterly earnings and sales
A: Annual earnings increases
N: New products, new management, new highs
S: Supply and demand
L: Leader or laggard
I: Institutional sponsorship
M: Market direction

Now let's take a closer look at these characteristics.

C: Most great stocks demonstrated superior earnings and sales before they launched their price runs. So it makes sense to buy stocks with large year-over-year increases in current quarterly earnings and sales, preferably 25 percent or more. The higher the better, particularly if that growth rate is accelerating (i.e., getting larger each quarter). In O'Neil's studies, stocks with strong quarterly earnings and sales growth had a higher probability of success.

A: Concentrate on stocks that have annual earnings growth in each of the prior three years of 25 percent or more.

N: Look for companies that have introduced new products or changed management or that bring something else new to the table that sets them apart from the competition. In addition, using technical analysis, look for stocks that have consolidated (i.e., moved sideways or traded in a range) for a while before breaking out to reach new price highs.

S: The stock market is all about supply and demand. Find stocks that are rising in price on rising volume, a signal that institutional investors might be buying. Trading volume should be at least 40 percent above average when a stock breaks out of a consolidation or base pattern. In addition, look for companies that buy back their own stock and for upper-level managers who privately own shares in their company—this means that they have a stake in its success.

L: Buy the strongest stocks in an industry group or sector—the leaders. There is no reason to buy weak stocks (the laggards) just because the price is lower. In particular, buy the strongest stocks in a good market (what technicians call *relative strength*). You want the leading stocks in the strongest industries. And those stocks should have a relative price strength rating of 80 or more (a statistic found only in *Investor's Business Daily*).

I: Buy stocks that are also owned by institutional investors such as pension funds, banks, and mutual funds. Stocks with strong institutional support are liquid, so they're easy to enter and exit. They're also less prone to big price swings than are thinly traded stocks.

M: Observe price and volume indicators to understand the strength and weakness of the market. Since three out of four growth stocks tend to follow the overall market trend, it's critical to know how the broader market is doing. Use stock charts to identify market tops and bottoms. Use technical analysis not to make predictions, but to understand what the market is doing right now. *Note:* I'll introduce stock charts and technical analysis in Chapter 13.

Some of the rules that O'Neil created go against human nature. For example, many people are obsessed with buying low and selling high. After all, everyone wants to get a bargain. But if you follow O'Neil's strategy, he asks why you would buy companies that are losing value.

If you think of the stock market as an auction, then his advice makes sense. When a once-great stock goes down in price, it's going down for a reason. Many people think they're getting a good deal, but they are actually buying weakening merchandise. Merchandise that is reduced in price is reduced for a reason. It's true that professional value investors with teams of analysts can find bargains. But most individual investors don't have the time to be value investors and find companies with potential at a low price.

If you are new to the stock market, you must start somewhere and CAN SLIM is a great place to start. What I like most about CAN SLIM is that it combines fundamental analysis with technical analysis. So when you're ready to buy individual stocks, you can use CAN SLIM to be sure that you are buying strong, leading stocks with upward potential. And learning to spot CAN SLIM traits helps you learn to recognize the very best stocks when they're launching their price run-ups.

And now, I have a special surprise. Mr. O'Neil graciously agreed to an interview.

Introducing William O'Neil

After William O'Neil joined the Air Force, he bought his first stock with only $500, which was all the money he had at the time. He experimented with a number of different strategies, and at first he didn't do very well. In fact, it took him two-and-a-half years to figure out how to make money in the stock market. He spent that time studying and learning everything he could about stocks. There was a lot of trial and error.

The books that influenced him the most were written by professional traders Gerald Loeb (*The Battle for Investment Survival*) and Jesse Livermore (*Reminiscences of a Stock Operator*). Their writings helped O'Neil develop the framework for many of his strategies.

At first, O'Neil simply bought the market leaders and thought that he had done well. In fact, he had only broken even. This is when he made an amazing discovery: He knew how to buy stocks, but he had no idea when to sell them. To solve this problem, he created a set of selling rules.

In 1962, his new selling rules told him to sell everything, which he did. He even made a little money selling short. When the market turned around in 1963, he invested all his cash ($3,000), borrowed another $2,000, and pyramided his $5,000 investment into a $200,000 windfall. With the money he made, he bought a seat on the New York Stock Exchange.

A few decades later, he founded *Investor's Business Daily* and wrote *How to Make Money in Stocks*.

Sincere: Are there other clues that show when a market reaches a top? Do you ever go by your instinct?

O'Neil: You start to see leading stocks falter and begin to sell off. If the winners can't buck a difficult market, that's a signal of weakness. Traders shouldn't go by instinct. Rather, they should look at what the market and individual stocks are telling them in terms of their price and volume action, and fundamentals.

Sincere: Have volume numbers changed since you first started investing?

O'Neil: Yes, there's more money in the market, more stocks, and more traders than there were decades ago, but the chart patterns remain the same. In an ideal, strong market, you're looking for stocks to make new price highs on heavy volume. You can see this action in charts, which are vital to timing any investment. The key is to watch what the market indexes and stocks are doing.

Sincere: How do you make money during market corrections?

O'Neil: Often, the safest place to be during a correction is on the sidelines in cash. But it's an interesting statistic that 72 percent of stocks that maintain a good base pattern during a correction are typically the first out of the gate when the market goes into an uptrend. So although you do not want to stay invested in a correction because three-quarters of growth stocks follow the market trend, it is an important signal to watch for stocks holding up against that downtrend.

Sincere: What did you learn most from trader Jesse Livermore?

O'Neil: Pyramiding, or averaging up in a stock, is one key area he followed. What Livermore meant is that you wade into a stock with your first purchase, but if the stock rises, you can buy a few more shares.

Sincere: What about market trends?

O'Neil: The M in CAN SLIM helps investors spot pivotal market trends. Don't invest in weak markets, since stocks get caught in the undertow. But CAN SLIM works to get you into good markets and signals when it is time to get out.

Sincere: Is there any particular economic indicator you watch?

O'Neil: Rather than look at individual economic indicators, we look at how the market reacts to those indicators. For instance, the monthly payroll report can be a big market mover.

Sincere: What else should investors do?

O'Neil: The most successful strategy is one that has rules, devoid of emotions. That's how an investor avoids falling in love with a stock. Investors need a strong plan to manage any scenario that might come up. Emotions can curb sound judgment.

Sincere: What was the most important lesson you learned from Bernard Baruch?

O'Neil: Don't be afraid to sell a stock that is rising and lock in your gains. Baruch did this regularly to achieve major success.

Sincere: If you had to choose three lessons for investors, what would they be?

O'Neil: Learn the rules. Learn to read charts. Study your mistakes.

Sincere: Are there other rules you learned that are not in your book?

O'Neil: We recently updated the book to also include 100 stock winners in chart form. That was something we realized could be critical for investors to study. Once you've gotten in the habit of reading charts, seeing patterns that resemble the big winners, you will improve your investing.

So to answer your question about adding anything new, this is not my system, but a historical analysis that proves how stocks build steam and are recognized and bought by the institutions. It's basically watching the market action as it happens using CAN SLIM as your guide.

That doesn't mean that markets don't have nuances—and that's why we're always studying markets to catch those. That means, for instance, that market conditions are somewhat unique each year, but the general rules are the same.

Sincere: Do you ever trade ETFs?

O'Neil: We're instituting some new features in this area because of the interest in ETFs. But growth stocks typically outperform other investing approaches, so CAN SLIM is an excellent guide for the individual investor.

What I Learned from CAN SLIM

After talking to Mr. O'Neil and studying CAN SLIM, I developed 26 rules.

1. You must have a set of buy-and-sell rules and stick to them.
2. You must cut losses at a predetermined amount such as 7 or 8 percent below the price paid for the stock. (For me, it's usually 5 percent, but sometimes more.) *Important:* Take a small loss now versus a potentially larger loss later.
3. Most people want to buy stocks at a lower price but often they are chasing after losers. Instead of buying stocks that are going down, buy stocks that are on the way up. Although it goes against human nature (buy high and sell higher) and you are paying more, you are getting higher-quality stocks. Your goal is not to buy at the cheapest price or at the low, but to buy at the right time when you have the best chance for success. Why buy stocks with weak earnings and a declining stock price? Don't buy stocks on the way down simply because they look cheap. O'Neil has another saying based on his research: Stocks making new highs tend to go higher, while stocks making new lows tend to go lower.
4. Be sure not to buy a stock that is extended too far past its ideal buy point, and be ready to sell if the stock starts to show signs of weakness or if the broader market goes into a correction. The key is to buy a stock at the right price as it is breaking out of a base or other key chart pattern. This right price is what O'Neil calls a "pivot point" or the ideal buy point.
5. Don't chase after stocks if you miss the initial move. Instead, look for other growth stocks.
6. Buy stocks that lead their industries or sectors. Buy the best stocks.

7. When you own a stock that falls 7 to 8 percent below the purchase price or is showing other warning signs, sell it. Some people do the opposite: They sell their winners and hold onto their losers—a huge mistake.
8. Buy stocks with increasing institutional ownership.
9. Rather than averaging down (buying more shares of a stock that is falling), average up: If a stock price rises after your initial purchase, consider buying a little more.
10. When there is a lot of excitement about a stock and it's all over the news, this is often the time to sell.
11. Earnings are extremely important, and positive earnings may attract institutional buyers, which in turn may increase the stock price. The bigger the increase, the better.
12. If you buy a stock and it climbs more than 20 percent in less than three weeks, hold onto it for at least eight weeks from the date you originally bought it—unless it flashes outright sell signals. Winners like that are the ones that can make the big money.
13. Don't buy low-priced stocks.
14. Use both fundamental and technical analysis.
15. If a company's earnings or sales growth rate decelerates, this is a sign of weakness.
16. Keep losses small and allow for big wins when you are right.
17. Some people place a bet on a stock and stubbornly stay with it until they lose all or most of their money because they refuse to act on sell signals or when the broader market is in a correction. If you can read charts, you can time your entry into the stock to increase your chances of buying at the ideal price. Try to recognize the right time to sell. This greatly improves the odds of success.
18. Diversification sounds good, but O'Neil says that six or seven individual stocks are sufficient. The number depends on the amount of money you have to invest. Just as important, how many stocks can you monitor effectively? The key to proper diversification is not to own too many stocks and lose control of your ability to track them.
19. Price/earnings (P/E) ratios typically are part of a value investor's research. But studies have shown that most big winners had high P/E ratios before making their big price run-ups.

20. During a bear market, sell and stay on the sidelines (or sell short).
21. When the leading stocks start to falter, watch out below.
22. Do not buy during a market correction because most stocks that break out of bases or try to launch new run-ups during a bear market have a difficult time climbing. While others are losing their shirts in a weak market, look for the strongest stocks that are forming solid base patterns. Then you'll be ready to buy when the correction ends and a new market uptrend begins.
23. In the later stages of a bull market, even the market leaders can lose steam and break down. And this may be a warning sign that the bull market is coming to an end.
24. History has shown that most bull markets last two to four years and are typically followed by a bear market or recession.
25. Always pay attention to the overall market and whether it's bullish or bearish.
26. Watch volume very closely. If a stock is rallying on heavy volume, this is a positive sign. On the flip side, if a stock falls sharply on strong volume, it is a negative sign.

Introducing John Bogle

I have another surprise. John Bogle also agreed to speak with me about the stock market.

John Bogle is the founder and former CEO of the Vanguard Group, Inc., which he founded in 1974. He is also the author of 10 books, including *The Little Book of Common Sense Investing* (Wiley) and *Common Sense on Mutual Funds* (Wiley). He is a huge proponent of buying and holding index mutual funds.

Sincere: When did you first come up with the idea of buying index funds?

Bogle: It goes back to 1951, when I was at Princeton University. I wrote my senior thesis on the mutual fund industry. I examined many funds and studied their data. From my research, which I admit was somewhat superficial, I concluded that it was difficult, if not impossible, for mutual funds to consistently outperform the market averages. For me, that's where it began.

Sincere: How did you start the first index fund at Vanguard?

Bogle: By the time Vanguard started in 1974, we were in an ideal position to bring out the world's first index fund. I was inspired by a 1974 article in the *Journal of Portfolio Management* by economist Paul Samuelson, who was one of the greatest economists of the twentieth century. He challenged anyone to find "brute evidence" that active managers can beat the market. He pleaded for the creation of an index fund. In 1975, my first major business decision at Vanguard was starting the world's first index mutual fund, and Dr. Samuelson was my greatest supporter. He followed up by writing a four-page article in *Newsweek,* in which he said that his prayers were answered. It was important for me to have his support.

Sincere: Did the mutual fund industry follow your lead?

Bogle: Not at first. There was a poster circulating around Wall Street that said, "Index Funds are Un-American!" The mutual fund industry didn't understand why anyone would want to be average. Also, most people in the industry were not looking to lower costs for investors; rather, their goal was to increase revenues for mutual fund management companies by gathering assets and raising fees. It wasn't until the 1990s that index funds started to grow.

Sincere: Why do you like indexing?

Bogle: Index funds take the cost out of the system and guarantee investors their fair share of stock market returns. It's simple, although for some people it might be boring.

Sincere: What do you think about ETF index funds?

Bogle: I don't know if I approve or disapprove. If you were to buy an ETF such as SPY (SPDR S&P 500) or VTI (Vanguard Total Stock Market ETF), there is no reason why you can't buy and hold. The cost of holding an ETF and what I call a traditional index fund, or TIF, is about the same. The difference is that with an ETF, you can trade all day long, which you cannot do with a traditional index fund. So we must ask ourselves this question: Is that an opportunity or a curse? I would say it's a curse. The idea of trading "all day long, in real time" is just silly.

Sincere: What do you think of ETFs?

Bogle: Basically, broad-based ETFs are fine as long as you don't trade them. But they are traded a lot, and primarily by institutions. Institutions, however, are a different breed of cat. They are often speculating on market changes and want temporary exposure to the market. In my opinion, ETFs are the greatest marketing innovation in mutual funds in this century, but I am dubious whether they are a great investment innovation. Unfortunately, marketing people don't worry whether ETFs are good for investors.

Sincere: Are there other problems with ETFs?

Bogle: One problem is that people can move from broad-based ETFs into narrowly focused, speculative ETFs with triple leverage. I call that the lunatic fringe. There's too much risk, and they are not diversified. These non-diversified ETFs have very speculative characteristics, none of which I like.

Sincere: You believe strongly in buy and hold. What if you see a bear market coming? Should you still hold?

Bogle: Yes. First, you should be properly diversified and your asset allocation must be right. Sixty percent stocks and 40 percent bonds is a good place to start. If you see a bear market developing in advance, you must get out at the height of the market, and jump back when it hits its low. But I don't know anyone who can tell you precisely when a bear market is going to begin, and I certainly can't tell you when it's going to end. So you have to be right twice. The chances of that are so small that you should just stick to your long-term investment plan. It's great advice to tell me to get out of stocks before a bear market. But can you drop me a note when it's time to get back in? I think investors should stay the course whether it's a bear market or not. Don't try to outsmart the market.

Sincere: What do you suggest?

Bogle: Don't pay too much attention to the daily gyrations of the stock market. If you have a diversified portfolio with low costs, simply stay the course. Yes, you would have been right if you got out at the high and back in at the low, but I not only don't know anybody who actually did so, I don't know anyone who knows anyone who did it.

Sincere: How should someone start with indexing?

Bogle: If you get out of college and are able to put a couple of hundred dollars away in an index fund, which is the only intelligent choice, you'll learn how the markets work. You'll learn what happens when prices go down, and learn about the wisdom of a buy-and-hold strategy. Don't try to time the market. Simply stick to a disciplined, long-term investment strategy. Invest whatever you can afford to save every month, and don't worry about what the market is doing. It doesn't matter. When the market suffers a 50 percent drop, people panic and think about getting out. Their emotions lead them in the wrong direction. Don't fall for that trap. Simply continue to invest every month without worrying about the momentary movement of stock prices. Just look at the quarterly statements and, over the course of an investment lifetime, you'll be overwhelmingly satisfied with your returns. You'll see that you fared much better than most other people who let their emotions get the better of them.

Sincere: Should you ever sell?

Bogle: Gradually, as you get into your 30s and 40s and you have more money at stake, you should begin to diversify some of your assets in equity index funds and invest in a bond index fund. You want to change your allocation gradually by reducing your stock position and building your bond position. Historically, bond index funds have generally had higher yields than stock index funds, although that will not always be the case.

Sincere: Should investors buy and hold individual stocks?

Bogle: If you are one of those rare, fortunate people who know how to pick winners, by all means you should definitely buy good stocks and forget indexing. But I don't know how to do that. The record is quite clear that, in many cases, what we thought were good stocks can turn out to be disasters. Look at it this way: People like to gamble, and investors are no exception. The math is the same on Wall Street as it is in Las Vegas. You bet on red, someone else bets on black, but in the long run, only the house wins. And Wall Street, the croupier in the middle, doesn't care what you do as long as you do something.

Sincere: What about investors who think they can beat the market?

Bogle: First, you should create a long-term investment portfolio with an appropriate mix of stock and bond index funds. This is your serious money account. It's the money you need for retirement. That should be 90 to 95 percent of your investable assets. It is very boring to watch, but exciting when you are ready to retire. Take the other 5 percent of your assets and use it as "funny money." I recommend creating a separate account for your funny money, and you can trade in that account to your heart's content. Many people have a gambling instinct, and in this account you can trade individual stocks. After five years, check out the returns and see if you actually beat the market. Did you? I think the chances are not quite zero, but maybe one or two percent that you did.

Sincere: Why doesn't everyone buy index funds?

Bogle: The idea of indexing is somewhat counterintuitive. It's the idea that no one is consistently better than the index. If you get a salesperson that says you shouldn't believe the index fund bunk, that their fund does better, it can be hard to resist. But they don't tell you that many active fund companies switch managers often. When you include all the additional expenses incurred by actively managed funds, what are the chances that all these asset managers can beat the market? I would say it's not zero, but maybe 0.0001 percent. But asset managers are great marketers, and they focus only on those funds that beat the market.

Sincere: Any final advice?

Bogle: In the long run, investment return is driven by economics, not emotion. Corporate value increases over time through dividend payments and earnings growth. In the very long run, stock market returns equal corporate returns. In the short term, all bets are off. Hang on for the long run and enjoy the returns that corporate America earns and will continue to earn.

Two More Wizards on Wall Street: Warren Buffett and Peter Lynch

William O'Neil and John Bogle are well-known investors, but two others have also reached legendary status. The first, familiar to most investors, is Warren Buffett.

Warren Buffett

If you ask professional investors to name the greatest investor of all time, most of them will probably name billionaire Warren Buffett. He is best known as the CEO of Berkshire Hathaway, a company that owns or has large investments in a number of businesses, including insurance, publishing, and manufacturing companies.

Benjamin Graham, the author of two value investment classics, *Security Analysis,* first published in 1934, and *Intelligent Investor,* influenced Buffett early in his life. Buffett later worked for Graham at Graham's brokerage firm, learning from the master how to manage investment portfolios and pick value stocks.

Buffett made a number of successful modifications to Graham's original strategies. He uses a stock's book value, P/E, and dividend yield, among other measurements, to calculate the company's fair value. He believes in buying a company for less than it's worth and patiently holding its stock for a lifetime.

Buffett strongly believes in buying stocks in companies that are simple and understandable. That's why he avoided investing in Internet stocks because he couldn't determine their true value. Most Internet companies had little or no earnings and sky-high P/E ratios. When Internet stocks were most popular (during the 1990s), several pros derided Buffett for not investing in these companies. In hindsight, Buffett was right, and he avoided the Internet stock bust.

Buffett earned a reputation for honesty and having a sense of humor. He was one of the first to point out that you should be cautious about investing in companies that play accounting games when they use stock options to compensate employees.

Many people have tried to emulate Buffett's successful buy-and-hold strategies. A number of excellent books have been written about his methods, most of which are based on common sense. The difficult part for most investors is learning how to value a business—something that Buffett has learned how to do after a lifetime of investment success.

Legendary Investor Peter Lynch

Peter Lynch ran the multibillion-dollar Fidelity Magellan Fund, which had a spectacular 29.2 percent average yearly return for over 20 years, the best record of any mutual fund manager in history. This is one of the reasons that Lynch has reached legendary status.

Lynch coined the phrase, "Invest in what you know," which suggests that people invest in stocks of companies with which they're familiar. He also suggested that investors go to the mall or workplace and observe what people are buying and which stores are busy. He said that is an excellent way for investors to get stock ideas.

He is the author of three best-selling books, *Learn to Earn, One Up on Wall Street*, and *Beating the Street*, all published by Simon & Schuster. In his books, he suggests ignoring the short-term ups and downs of the market and focusing on finding successful companies that are likely to grow over the long term (many years).

The main point is that when Lynch buys a stock, he is investing in a company. Therefore, if a company's profits go up, the stock price will go up. According to Lynch, there is a 100 percent correlation.

For Lynch, the key to being a successful investor is finding companies that are doing something right, are profitable, and are clearly superior to the competition. He was able to identify winning companies in the early days that had excellent products. He was an early investor in Walmart, Dunkin' Donuts, and Stop & Shop. The stocks of all three companies did extremely well, rewarding their investors.

Lynch is known for visiting the companies whose stock he owned. For example, he went to automobile dealers to check their cars and minivans to see which company had the best products. For Lynch, knowing the stock price is not as important as checking the story and knowing the company's fundamentals.

Lynch takes a dim view of those who use the market for gambling and speculation. "A stock is not a lottery ticket," he told me in an interview.

He also doesn't make stock market predictions. "I'd love to know what will happen in the future," he said. "In fact, I've been trying to get next year's *Wall Street Journal* for the past 40 years. I'd pay an extra dollar for it. I have no idea what the market will do over the next one or two years."

Lynch takes market corrections in stride, including bear markets, when the market goes down by 20 to 25 percent. "If you understand what companies you own and who their competitors are, you're in good shape. You don't panic if the market goes down and the stock goes down. If you don't understand what you own and don't understand what a company does and it falls by half, what should you do? If you haven't done your research, you might as well call a psychic hotline for investment advice."

According to Lynch, there are always opportunities in the market if you take the time to look for them. He believes that people should have a basic understanding of how the stock market works, advice you should pass onto your children.

Trader Jesse Livermore

Another Wall Street legend is speculator Jesse Livermore, whose exploits are well known to many traders. His view of the market was exactly opposite to that of Warren Buffett and Peter Lynch. Rather than holding stocks for the long term, he speculated on the short-term price movements of stocks. The stock market was like the Wild West in the late nineteenth century, and Livermore took advantage of the lack of rules and regulations. And yet, the heart of the stock market is nearly the same as it was in Livermore's day.

There is little doubt that Jesse Livermore was one of the world's most successful stock traders. While still a teenager, Livermore quit school to become a "board boy" for a stock brokerage firm. (Before computers, board boys updated stock and bond prices manually on a large chalkboard.)

The story of Jesse Livermore's life and the lessons he learned about trading can be found in his book, *Reminiscences of a Stock Operator,* originally published in 1923. Although the author is given as Edwin Lefevre, most believe that Livermore wrote the book himself. It is still one of the most popular and valuable books ever written on speculating in the stock market.

Livermore (speaking through the fictional character of Larry Livingston) complains how he made a series of mistakes that cost money, although he never lost it all (at first). His losses were painful but educational. "There is nothing like losing all you have in the world for teaching you what not to do," he says. "And when you know what not to do in order not to lose money, you begin to learn what to do in order to win."

After going broke three times in less than three years, Livermore had this advice: "Being broke is a very efficient educational agency." He said that you learn little from your winners because they take care of themselves, but the losers teach you lessons that will last a lifetime. The key is not to make the same mistake twice.

Livermore spent much of his time trading in "bucket shops." (Bucket shops were unlicensed brokerages that have been described as "gambling dens.") Starting with a $5 investment when he was 15 years old, Livermore became so successful at trading stocks that he was banned from most bucket shops by the time he was 20. He was forced to wear disguises and use fake names to trade. Nevertheless, this gave him the opportunity to watch how other traders manipulated the markets.

After closely studying the markets, he created a successful rule-based trading system. As he became wealthier, Livermore made most of his trades from an elaborate secret office that was connected by telephone to the New York Stock Exchange.

Much of the money that Livermore made came from shorting stocks (he was famously bearish). He made a lot of enemies on his roller-coaster ride, and he was often opposed by some of the country's most influential financial leaders. Keep in mind that many of the tactics that Livermore used are now illegal, including manipulating stocks by using inside information and arranging with reporters to have incorrect information published. (One of his tricks was to wait until he had a profit on a stock, and then reveal to an influential reporter that this particular stock was a great buy. When the stock went higher, he immediately unloaded his position in classic pump and dump style.)

In his book, Livermore said that he believed he had found the secret to successful trading. He was very excited about his discovery, which he shares: "After spending years on Wall Street and after making and losing millions of dollars I want to tell you this: It was never my thinking that made the big money for me. It was always my sitting. Got that? My sitting tight! It is no trick at all to be right on the market. I've known many traders who were right at exactly the right time, and began buying and selling stocks when prices were at the very level that should show the greatest profit. And their experience invariably matched mine, that is, they made no real money out of it. Traders who can be both right and sit tight are uncommon. I found it one of the hardest things to learn. But it is only after a stock operator has grasped this that he can make the big money."

Another lesson that is hard for most people to learn is how to take losses. Many people are just unwilling to sell stock positions that are losing money. Here's how Livermore put it: "A loss never bothers me after I take it. I forget it overnight. But being wrong, not taking the loss, that is what does damage to the pocketbook and to the soul."

As you already know, buying stock based on tips is the most common novice error. Even Livermore was vulnerable to tips from well-meaning friends, and they always caused him grief. He wrote, "Tips! How people want tips! They crave not only to get them, but to give them." He said that trading on tips cost him hundreds of thousands of dollars, especially the kind given on the street by casual acquaintances. "I know from experience that nobody can give me a tip or a series of tips that will make more money for me than my own judgment."

Much of Livermore's success came from observing people, individual stocks, and the overall market. (It did help that he had a photographic memory.) Here's how Livermore summarized his trading strategy: "I have found that experience is apt to be a steady payer in this game and that observation gives you the best tips of all." And according to Livermore: "Not even a world war can keep the stock market from being a bull market when conditions are bullish, or a bear market when conditions are bearish. All a trader needs to know to make money is how to appraise conditions." Studying general market conditions was one of his greatest discoveries, he claimed.

Livermore also had a Livermore moment when he discovered the value of following the market trend. "Obviously, the thing to do was to be bullish in a bull market and bearish in a bear market. Sounds silly, doesn't it? But I had to grasp that general principle firmly before I saw that to put it into practice really meant to anticipate probabilities. It took me a long time to trade on those lines."

Livermore used a number of methods to buy and sell stocks. One of his methods was to buy as soon as a stock made a new high (what William O'Neil learned from Livermore), which Livermore said would certainly bring him profits.

Livermore wrote, "I have often said that to buy on a rising market is the most comfortable way of buying stocks. Now, the point is not so much to buy as cheap as possible or get short at the top prices, but to buy or sell at the right time." Livermore adds that he often scales into a stock as it rises. He called it "pyramiding," and it was the key to his success in the market.

He also studied prices for clues to market direction. "Prices, as we know, will either move up or down according to the resistance they encounter. For purposes of easy explanation, we will say that prices, like everything else, move along the line of least resistance."

Livermore warned that although his method sounds easy to implement, you always have to be on guard against your natural impulses: fear, hope, and greed and, most important, "a swelled head." Often, when the market was being uncooperative, Livermore would take a vacation.

Not long after making and losing his fourth million-dollar fortune (he made his first million when he was 31), Livermore walked into a hotel hatcheck room and shot himself in the head. Although he had once been worth millions, dated glamorous actresses, and owned a number of houses and boats, at the time of his death at age 63, his estate was reported to be worth less than $10,000.

And now, you will enter the most challenging part of the book: learning about fundamental and technical analysis. Learning how to use these tools will help you determine when to buy a stock and, just as important, when to sell.

PART FOUR

DECIDE WHICH STOCKS TO BUY OR SELL

11

It's Really Fundamental: How to Analyze Companies

Now that you have been introduced to some money-making strategies, you probably want to know which stocks to pick, and how to evaluate them so you can make better investments. This is the chapter that will help you choose and evaluate stocks using fundamental analysis. Other chapters in this section show you how to use technical analysis to evaluate stocks.

Let's pretend that you are a doctor dealing with a new patient who has come to see you for a checkup. You might begin by asking questions, have the patient fill out a questionnaire, ask about his or her medical history, and ask whether anyone in the family has any medical problems. You will probably have a checklist. If you relate this preparation to the stock market, this is *fundamental analysis*.

You might also take an Electrocardiogram (EKG) of the patient. By looking at the EKG, you can identify potential problems or clear the patient. Looking at the patient's EKG is similar to looking at a chart on the stock market. This is called *technical analysis*.

I'll be honest with you: For some of you, these concepts will be difficult to grasp, but they're also among the most important for stock trading. After all, if you jump into the market with a fistful of stock ideas without knowing if the stocks are a good value, you could lose money.

Also, by using fundamental or technical analysis, you can find your own stocks or evaluate stocks you heard about rather than relying on tips from someone on TV or acquaintances. Learning how to evaluate stocks is a time-consuming skill you should learn.

As you'll discover, fundamental and technical analysis are more art than science. Although everyone is looking at the same data, the hard part is interpreting the data to generate useful conclusions. Here's something else you should know: Even when you are using some of the best software and hardware, there is no guarantee you will make money.

You really have two choices: You can research the company, its earnings, and balance sheet. That's fundamental analysis. Or you can study price and volume and look at market indicators on charts. That's technical analysis. (A third choice is to let others do it for you.)

In my opinion, you should use both methods because each has strengths as well as weaknesses. By using both fundamental and technical analysis, you will become a much better and more knowledgeable investor.

And now, let's get started learning about fundamental analysis.

Understanding Fundamental Analysis

The most common question that beginners ask is: How do you find stocks to buy? It's a very good question. If you *go long* by buying shares of stock in a company, you expect the stock price to go up. But if you make a poor choice, then the stock is far more likely to go down, and you will probably lose money.

So how do people choose which stocks to buy? One of the most popular methods is using *fundamental analysis*. Fundamental analysis is the study of the underlying data that affect a corporation. In other words, you learn everything you can about the health of the company that issues the stock.

For example, you might look at how much the company is earning, study the balance sheet, and look at the *price/earnings ratio* (P/E).

Although there is a lot of data to examine, I chose the most important data that you need to understand and analyze.

Some of you may find that fundamental analysis is all you need in order to be a successful investor. After all, understanding and applying fundamental stock analysis helped make investor Warren Buffett a billionaire (along with his other wise investment decisions).

In addition, successful mutual fund managers such as Peter Lynch have used fundamental analysis to find high-quality stocks selling for bargain prices. If you want to learn about the stock market, you must have at least a basic understanding of fundamental analysis. It is worth your time to study it.

Note: You can find company fundamentals on a number of websites such as Bloomberg, Briefing.com, *Investor's Business Daily*, Market-Watch, Yahoo! Finance, and Google Finance, to name a few. You can also find fundamental information about companies on your brokerage firm's website, but also read the company's annual and quarterly reports. If possible, get the 10-Q filings because they contain information that is often not available elsewhere.

If you are going to go this route, do it right. Your task is to analyze this data if you expect to find undervalued stocks to buy or overvalued stocks to sell.

> *Hint:* Be aware that many people, including highly paid, professional money managers, spend every working day using fundamental analysis. Even so, most pros do not beat the major market indexes each year. As a beginner, even if you don't have the time to study fundamental analysis, you do want to learn the basics. So let's get started!

Fundamental Analysis: An Overview

When you buy a stock on the basis of fundamental analysis, you are not simply buying a piece of paper. You are buying a piece of a corporation. If you're going to buy a stock, you should find out as much as you can about the company. This is the essence of fundamental analysis: You study the corporation to decide whether it is a worthwhile investment compared to every other stock.

Many of the factors (such as the company's assets and liabilities, earnings, and amount of debt) can be found in the balance sheet, a brief financial report of the corporation that is discussed shortly. By using fundamental analysis, you hope to find stocks that offer you the best chance for profits. You want to buy a stock whose price is reasonable when compared with its earnings—what fundamental analysts call *fair value*. Note: It takes experience and skill to determine the fair value of a stock.

Fundamental analysis is a popular method of determining whether a stock is a good buy or is better left alone. If you have done your homework and closely studied all aspects of a corporation, and if your analysis is correct, you should be rewarded with a higher stock price (but there are no guarantees).

Keep in mind that fundamental analysis is only a tool to help you find and evaluate which stocks offer good value. Like anything related to the stock market, just because you use fundamental analysis doesn't mean that you'll make a lot of money in the market. However, it does mean that on average, you will own quality stocks, and that means you have a better-than-average chance to find success. The more methods you learn, however, the better. This will also give you a chance to determine whether fundamental analysis is right for you.

The Concepts Behind Fundamental Analysis

To get you started with fundamental analysis, let's take a look at some of the key concepts behind this technique.

Know the Company's Business

The first thing an investor has to determine when using fundamental analysis is what industry to look at. If we are in the middle of a recession, when jobs are scarce and people are struggling to stay out of debt, you might look at recession-proof industries like food, oil, and retail. Once the country is out of the doldrums and jobs are plentiful, you may want to look at growing and expanding industries such as technology. You want to find companies that will lead the market higher.

Another way to get stock ideas and find good companies is by going to the mall. As you know, Peter Lynch got many of his stock ideas by watching where his children shopped. If you go to the mall and The Gap, Apple, Sears, or Starbucks is filled with shoppers, observe whether they are walking out with packages or are leaving empty-handed. This will give you a clue whether these stores are making money. You can also talk to the store manager, employees, or customers for additional clues. Also, look for exciting businesses that are new. This is one of the best ways to discover future success stories in the early stages (think of the early investors in Microsoft, Home Depot, and McDonald's).

This doesn't mean that you should run out and buy stock in one of these companies. Nor does it mean that all your stocks should be in the retail sector. Nevertheless, you can use fundamental analysis to find out everything you can about the company. You can also read the annual report, call investor relations for an investment packet, and log on to the company website for additional information.

Note: Much of this is marketing material, which will give you little useful information. Later, you'll learn how to find the important data, i.e., sales and revenue results. That will be a lot more helpful than reading sales pitches.

Bottom line: You don't want to invest any money in a stock without understanding the company's business and forming an opinion about the future success of the business. Ideally, the business will be simple and understandable with good long-term prospects. Also, compare the company with its competitors, and be especially alert to thriving newcomers. In addition to finding companies to invest in, you should also look at companies in profitable industries such as technology, pharmaceuticals, biomedical, and retail. Then find and analyze data for the leading companies in those sectors.

Identify the Leading Company

Once you have identified an industry you want to invest in, you want to choose companies that are stronger and more profitable than their competition. Let's say you want to invest in the retail sector because you believe (after careful research) that people will flock to discount stores.

What stores come to mind? Walmart? Home Depot? Target? Lowe's? Exactly. Choose the stores that have name brand recognition and that advertise heavily. These companies are called *industry leaders.* If people are buying the company's products, the company's earnings will go up, which should cause the stock price to rise. To find industry leaders, you want to look for companies that have superior sales and earnings with little or no debt. Also look for newer companies that do not yet have stores all over the country. If you find a growing and successful business at this early stage, you may discover a great growth opportunity. Unfortunately, not all smaller companies expand, and some disappear, so you must do your homework.

The financial newspaper *Investor's Business Daily* rates the relative price strength (RS) of stocks in leading industries, giving them a score between 1 and 99. A relative price strength rating higher than 90 is considered excellent. (Note: Relative price strength compares a stock's price performance over the next 12 months with other stocks in the IBD database.)

You can also find information about industry leaders in the *Value Line Investment Survey,* which can be found at the public library or online with a paid subscription. (The *Value Line Investment Survey* has loads of information about individual stocks condensed onto a single page. Nearly all the basic fundamental information you need to know about a stock can be found in this periodical.)

Talk to the Managers

Many large institutional investors who use fundamental analysis talk to the CEO and company managers to get a feel for how the corporation is being run. Ideally, when they speak to the CEO, they can ask how the business is doing, where the company will be spending its money, and who its competitors are. This can help give insights about the corporation.

Because professional fund managers own (or may purchase) millions of shares in the company, they have access to upper management. The pros want to invest in companies with experienced, innovative managers who have a vision for the future. They try to avoid companies that have too much debt, are losing business to competitors, and have other liabilities (such as lawsuits) that can affect earnings.

As an individual investor, however, it is highly unlikely that you will be able to sit down with the CEO or upper management to share a drink and a game of golf and to try to find out exactly what is going on in the corporation. And even if you could, it is doubtful that the CEO would say anything negative about the corporation. This is why management interviews are somewhat controversial. In fact, some institutional investors would rather study the balance sheet than talk with managers (and I know because they told me).

Observe Company Insiders

According to the SEC (Securities and Exchange Commission), officers and directors of a corporation who have access to proprietary information and people who own more than 10 percent of the corporation's stock are considered *corporate insiders.*

You can get clues to how a stock will do by looking at whether insiders are buying or selling stock in their own company. One way to find out what insiders are doing is by looking at financial websites. Also look at the SEC's website, www.sec.gov, which manages the EDGAR (electronic data gathering analysis and retrieval) database. It contains many fascinating financial documents about the actions of insiders.

Some investors have created strategies that involve copying insiders. After all, insiders "should" be more knowledgeable about the future prospects of the company than others. On the other hand, there are problems with tracking insider transactions. Sometimes insiders buy or sell for personal reasons that have nothing to do with what is happening in the company. In addition, because of the way insider transactions are reported, you may not find out what insiders are doing until it is too late (insider reports are sometimes delayed by up to three months).

The Balance Sheet: How Is the Company Doing?

A *balance sheet* is a report of the financial condition of a business, including items that only an accountant could love. And yet, to really understand the company you plan to invest in, you should study its balance sheet. The balance sheet tells you how the business has been doing from its first year in business.

Often, many people buy stocks without taking the time to read the balance sheet. Just remember this: You shouldn't invest thousands of dollars in a company unless you know a few facts about it, like how much the company earns, how much it spends, and how much it owes. You also want to compare these numbers with the competition. That is the whole point of fundamental analysis: finding the best, or one of the better, companies. When you have found out the truth about a company's earnings, expenses, and debt, you'll have a better idea of whether you should buy its stock.

The balance sheet is found at the back of a company's annual report. Let's take a quick look at some of the items on a balance sheet (which by no means includes everything):

1. Assets (what the company owns, such as cash, property, equipment, real estate, and accounts receivable)
2. Liabilities (what the company owes, such as declared and unpaid dividends and accounts payable)
3. Shareholders' equity, or net worth (assets minus liabilities)

Simply put, a balance sheet is a list of everything a company owns and everything it owes. This gives shareholders a snapshot of the company's finances. The best way to study a balance sheet is to compare it to the balance sheets of other companies in the same industry. In addition, you should look at the balance sheet of previous years to get an idea of where the company has been and where it might be going.

As long as the company is not hiding debt or liabilities (not something you will know at first), the balance sheet gives you a glimpse of its financial condition. However, reading a balance sheet takes skill because some companies (the kind you don't want to buy) hide their expenses and debt while exaggerating their earnings. Hint: If you are a conservative investor, stick with well-known companies that pay dividends and are listed on the major stock exchanges. It is unlikely (although possible) they will be hiding debt or liabilities.

For example, only a few knowledgeable investors figure out that the balance sheets of failing companies don't add up. Upper management at some of these companies often gives extremely distorted views of the true financial picture. By the time you find out a company is going bankrupt, it is usually too late. (This is more common with penny stocks but in reality any company can go bankrupt.)

Here's some wise advice from Warren Buffett: He never invests in a company when he doesn't understand how it makes its money. So if you're confused by how a certain company makes money, even after studying the balance sheet, invest your money elsewhere.

Income Statement: How Is the Company Doing Now?

While the balance sheet tells you about the company from its first year, the *income statement* tells you about the company's current year. It contains a lot of useful information such as the company's sales, operating expenses, and earnings.

The first line of the income statement gives the company's sales or revenue (also referred to as the *top line*). Look to see if the company's earnings and revenues are increasing when compared to those in earlier years. For example, if you are a growth investor, look for companies whose earnings are increasing by 15 percent or more each year.

The next section of the income statement gives operating expenses. These are the costs of doing business, such as salaries, advertising, training employees, and buying new computers, etc. There is usually also a line for research and development (R&D), which is the cost of developing and investing in new products.

The next three sections of the income statement describe the company's income. Have you wondered where the phrase "bottom line" comes from? This refers to a company's net income (which happens to be on the bottom line of the income statement). After paying all expenses, how much money did the company make? This is net income.

The Annual Report

For many people, there isn't anything more boring than reading the annual report, issued by every publicly owned corporation. These reports are often long, sometimes 80 pages or more, and contain important financial documents such as the balance sheet and income statement. They also contain information regarding the company's growth strategy, marketing and advertising plans, sales strategy, and any potential risks that could affect the company.

Often, there is a letter from the CEO about the steps he or she is taking to make the business more profitable, how the company has performed, and business strategies. Unless you are an accountant or a lawyer, it could easily take you all day to wade through the entire report. Besides, it often contains public relations fluff. Knowledgeable pros have learned to focus only on the information in the report they believe is important and ignore the rest. It takes experience to learn what items are important. Hint: Earnings and revenues are the first items you should study.

Almost all companies tend to highlight the positive aspects of their business while minimizing the negative. Some of the most fascinating tidbits can be found in the footnotes. This is where you may learn about perceived risks, ongoing legal issues, and other problems. The more negative information in the footnotes, the more cautious you should be. It's a red flag if a company appears to be hiding negative information.

Note: Well-known companies with strong balance sheets usually don't hide negative information in the fine print.

Although it takes time to read the entire annual report, it's worth your while to understand where you are putting your money. If you are a long-term investor, you want to learn whether or not the company is making money, whether its debt is rising or falling, and if management has a successful business plan.

Note: Most of the information you need to study can be found online, so annual reports are not as essential as they were in the past. Nevertheless, if you are investing money into a business, I recommend that you research the company, which includes understanding the contents of the annual report.

Note: Once you buy the company's stock, your brokerage firm will automatically send the company's annual report to you. Even if you don't own shares, you can call the company (investor relations) and ask for a free copy of the annual report.

. . . .

Now that you have been introduced to ways to analyze companies, let's go one step further. Next, you will learn about the tools that fundamental analysts use before buying or selling a stock.

Fundamental Analysis: Tools and Tactics

Fundamental analysts use a number of tools to evaluate and compare the stocks of a variety of businesses. After all, before buying a stock, you want to be sure that the company is of good quality and is a good value. Investors who primarily use fundamental analysis to choose stocks typically use a variety of tools to decide which stocks to pick. Although there are dozens of fundamental indicators and ratios, I introduce you to the ones that are the most important.

For example, one of the most useful pieces of fundamental information is the EPS, or *earnings per share.*

Earnings per Share (EPS): One Key to Choosing a Good Stock

No matter how good you think a corporation is or how much you love its managers, if the company isn't earning money, or if it is not earning enough to satisfy Wall Street, eventually its stock price will fall. This is why earnings per share (EPS) are so important. You can find this information at the bottom of the company's income statement, below net income. (Calculate EPS by dividing a company's after-tax profit by the number of the company's outstanding shares.)

Although reading balance sheets provides interesting clues, what you are primarily looking for are earnings (and revenue). If a company's earnings are growing each year and are expected to grow in the future, its stock is one you might consider buying. (Note: Later I'll show you how the pros estimate future earnings.)

Fortunately, you can quickly find up-to-date EPS on any number of financial websites, such as Yahoo! Finance, or in periodicals such as *Barron's,* the *Wall Street Journal,* MarketWatch, Google Finance, and Morningstar.com. The financial newspaper *Investor's Business Daily* also ranks the relative strength of earnings per share growth (EPS) on a scale of 1 to 99 (with 99 being the strongest and 1 the weakest).

> *Hint:* You can also type the stock symbol followed by the word "earnings" in to a search engine. For example, if you type "IBM earnings," a list of all the websites with IBM's earnings will be displayed. Be sure to check the dates because the search will pull up old information as well as current.

Note: Knowing the earnings is one part of the puzzle that we call the stock market. The other part is the market price of the stock (since we don't want to overpay). I'll discuss stock prices later in this chapter.

If a company is earning more money than it did in the past, it is often rewarded with a higher stock price (higher earnings and a higher P/E ratio). That's why it's so useful to compare the company's current earnings with those of the previous quarter or the previous year to determine the earnings growth rate. (Because some companies are seasonal, quarter-to-quarter comparisons are not as useful as year-to-year comparisons.)

Note: In my opinion, if you wanted to choose the most important fundamental measurement, I would say that you should look at a company's earnings.

The Earnings Estimates Game

In addition to the earnings per share, *stock analysts* (people who are paid to independently research corporations and make buy or sell recommendations on stocks) make estimates or predictions of companies' future earnings.

Often, a stock will rise on the *expectation* that the company's earnings will grow in the future. If a company beats analysts' estimates, the stock price usually performs well. If a company misses analysts' estimates, even by as little as a penny, the stock price usually falls. Sometimes a company will beat analysts' published estimates but not beat the "whisper number," an unofficial earnings estimate that is generally not made public. CEOs are under extreme pressure to beat the earnings estimates because they earn bonuses for good performance for each quarter. Fortunately, most CEOs are not that shortsighted, and do care about the long-term prospects of the company and the shareholders.

Since companies do not want to miss estimates, which can hurt the stock price, they tend to guide analysts to the most conservative estimates. It's like a game that I call, "Beat the Estimate." If analysts' estimates are on the low side and the number beats the estimates, it generates lots of positive publicity, and the stock price tends to rise.

On the other hand, if a company doesn't meet analysts' earnings expectations for the quarter, the stock could get severely punished. The last thing that anyone on Wall Street wants is a surprise, especially if it is bad news.

For example, if a company is expected to earn $0.10 per share in earnings and it earns $0.15 per share (beating the estimates by 50 percent), it's highly likely the stock price will please its shareholders. On the other hand, if a company is expected (based on analysts' reports) to earn $0.10 per share but misses by a penny, more than likely, the stock will decline.

The Stock Analysts

Here's how the stock analyst game is played: The investment banking divisions of major brokerage firms are paid big sums by their clients, so they often encourage the firms' analysts to be bullish on the companies that the firms represent. This is why analysts rarely say anything controversial or negative about a current or future client.

Basically, members of the investment banking group are cheerleaders for the companies they represent, and the marketing department doesn't want you (the investor) to sell stock in companies it represents. That is why there are so many "buy" recommendations on Wall Street, and very few "sells."

That is one reason why many of the full-service brokerage firms that help new companies go public are constantly issuing buy recommendations for stock in the companies they represent. Do you really think they are going to say anything negative about these companies?

More than likely, they will always put a buy rating on the stock, and if it's a really terrible company, instead of a strong buy, they might have it as a simple buy. In the wacky world of Wall Street, even a downgrade from strong buy to buy is significant.

There are many lessons to be learned from the games analysts play. If you are going to invest in the stock market, it is important that you understand how upgrades and downgrades influence a stock's price, and that you learn about the incestuous relationship that analysts have with the investment banking divisions of the brokerage companies. Because of negative publicity over this relationship, analysts' estimates have less power to move stocks than they did in the past. Because so many retail investors got burned by buying stocks based on analyst recommendations, many stopped listening. Nevertheless, analysts still have a large influence on stock prices.

The SEC has talked about eliminating the conflict of interest that exists between investment bankers and the analysts in the research departments of brokerages. Until the system is changed, however, you usually can't trust what many analysts say about stocks.

Most professional investors hire teams of analysts to come up with their own evaluation of the company and its business model. As a beginning investor, you can't be expected to independently evaluate a company. Fortunately, there are a few tools that can give you clues to whether a stock is under-or overvalued. The most well known is the price/earnings ratio (P/E), which you'll read about next.

Understanding Stock Ratios

There are a number of fundamental tools that can help investors determine whether a stock is a good value. A few of these tools include the P/E ratio, PEG, P/S, and ROE.

The Price/Earnings (P/E) Ratio: The Granddaddy of Stock Ratios

Many people use the price/earnings (P/E) ratio to get a quick idea of whether a stock price is reasonable. When you divide the stock price by the company's earnings per share, you end up with a P/E ratio (also known as the P/E *multiple*) that can help you determine whether a stock is fairly valued. Many people think that the P/E ratio is the most effective way to measure a stock. Actually, the P/E ratio is just one of many tools you can use to help you decide what stocks to buy. And now, let's take a closer look at how to use the P/E ratio.

For example, a stock that sells for $20 per share and earned $2 last year has a *trailing* P/E of 10 ($20 divided by $2). It's a *trailing* P/E because it uses earnings from the previous year. If a $20 stock were expected to earn $4 next year, it would have a *forward* P/E of 5 ($20 divided by $4). Forward P/E is using analysts' estimates of what will happen in the future. The great thing about the P/E ratio is that you can easily and quickly compare individual stocks with one another, with other stocks in their sector, or with the overall market. How does that help you? If you track the P/E of individual stocks, you will be able to see which stocks appear over- or undervalued (according to the P/E ratio). Using the P/E ratio is an excellent place to begin your fundamental research.

In fact, some investors decide whether to buy a stock based primarily on its P/E ratio. For example, some *value investors* (bargain hunters looking for stocks of high-quality companies that are selling for a reasonable price) prefer to buy stocks with low P/Es. (Warren Buffett, for example, once said that he only buys companies with trailing P/Es of 10 or less.) Nevertheless, although the P/E is useful, it should not be the only reason that you buy a stock.

Also, don't obsess too much on the actual number. To repeat, it's more important to compare the P/E of a stock with those of other stocks in its industry. In general, you can use the P/E to determine quickly if a stock is cheap or expensive when compared with its peers and the overall market.

As mentioned earlier, *growth investors* (aggressive buyers looking for stocks in companies whose sales or earnings are growing rapidly) don't mind buying stocks with high P/Es because they expect the companies' earnings to improve significantly in the future. If a stock has a P/E of 50 but is growing by 60 percent a year, the stock could be a bargain. Everyone loves rapidly growing businesses, and the shares demand a premium price, or a higher P/E ratio.

Nevertheless, basing your stock decisions on what a company's earnings might be in the future has backfired on many investors. In particular, analysts' expectations concerning future earnings have often been overly optimistic. Once again, if you have a sound reason for being optimistic about the future of a business, based on your own observations, that is a reason to own the stock.

There are many misconceptions about the P/E ratio. Just because a stock's P/E is low doesn't mean that you should buy the stock. And just because the P/E is high doesn't mean that the stock should be avoided (although the risk is higher).

Note: Pay attention to the P/E of the entire market. Typically, the P/E of the S&P 500 hovers around 15, its historical average. If it spikes higher, perhaps the market is overvalued. And if it drops well below 15, perhaps the market is undervalued.

Bottom line: Consider the P/E as a useful clue, but it is not wise to put real money into the market based solely on a stock's P/E or the market's P/E.

Price/Earnings/Growth (PEG): Taking the P/E One Step Farther

The P/E ratio is quite useful, but it doesn't take into account future earnings potential. This is what the price/earnings/growth (PEG) ratio is designed to do. To calculate the PEG, instead of simply dividing the stock price by the earnings (as you do for the P/E), divide the P/E by the anticipated rate of earnings growth for the company. For example, if a company has a P/E of 20 and an annual earnings growth rate of

10 percent, the PEG will be 2 (20 P/E divided by 10 annual earnings growth rate = 2).

The PEG allows you to take into account both the P/E and the company's growth rate in determining the value of a company. Many people feel that the PEG is more accurate than the P/E because it takes future growth into account.

A guideline for PEG users is as follows: A stock with a PEG of less than 0.50 is desirable (undervalued). A stock with a PEG between 0.50 and 1 is good (fair value). A stock with a PEG higher than 1 is not recommended, especially if the PEG is over 2 (overvalued).

Important: Remember, these are only guidelines, not absolute rules.

Warning: You should use the PEG as only one piece of a larger calculation. Do not decide to buy a stock based solely on the PEG (or any other single number). For the most complete and accurate calculation, it is suggested that you use the PEG to compare stocks within the same industry.

The problem with the PEG, like the forward P/E, is that you are basing calculations on earnings estimates, which have historically been unreliable. This is why it is so important that you use a variety of tools before deciding to buy or sell a stock.

Price/Sales (P/S) Ratio: Used to Uncover Revenue

Because P/E ratios are generally useless when examining companies that have no current earnings, some investors use the price/sales (P/S) ratio to help evaluate a stock. The reasoning is that although earnings can be tweaked, you can't play with revenue. With the P/S ratio, you compare price to sales revenue.

To calculate the P/S, divide the company's market capitalization by the total sales revenue booked for the previous year. Many mutual fund managers that I interviewed told me that the P/S is more reliable than the P/E or the PEG. And in fact, the P/S worked for many years. It was especially useful in valuing a stock relative to its own past performance, other companies, or the market.

But things change, and so do indicators. I also interviewed the creator of the P/S ratio, *Forbes* columnist and author Ken Fisher. "I don't think the P/S ratio has the power it used to have," he says. "When I was working on the P/S, there was no data written about it, so it was an exciting discovery. At the time, before the Internet, it was expensive to find the P/S of individual stocks."

Now, because anyone can get the P/S of a stock, it lost some of its luster, according to Fisher. He says that like many indicators, it worked for a period of time, but then stopped working during certain market environments.

It's an important lesson to remember. Although indicators are useful tools, be flexible when using them. Don't put real money in the market simply because an indicator is flashing a "go" signal. Use other indicators as well as your own judgment before investing.

Return on Equity (ROE): Measuring the Financial Health of a Company

Return on equity (ROE) is a tool that helps measure how effectively a company is being managed. Some fund managers consider ROE one of the most important measures of a company's overall financial performance. Calculate ROE by dividing net income by net worth. Note that this ratio is not as clear-cut as others because you must rely on subjective variables to calculate manager efficiency.

In general, the higher the ROE, the more effective the company is at using its resources and the more productive the management team is. In other words, ROE gives you an idea of how well the company is managed. The goal is to look for companies with a rising ROE and growing earnings.

Other Stock Measurements

There are many other fundamental stock measurements, including return on investment (ROI), debt-to-equity ratio, price-to-book ratio (P/B), return on assets (ROA), cash flow per share, and dividend yield.

The purpose of many of these fundamental tools is to help an investor decide whether a business is a good value compared to its stock price. (Note: If you want to learn even more about fundamental analysis, I list a number of books in Chapter 18.)

The Problem with Fundamental Analysis

I wish I could tell you that all you need to know are the fundamentals and you can pick winning stocks. Unfortunately, analyzing the market is like solving a jigsaw puzzle.

The biggest problem with fundamental analysis is that even if the company fundamentals are superb, the stock price can still go down. As you learned, the market goes up and down for a variety of reasons, and it's not always because of fundamentals. Supply and demand, fear and hope, and price and volume all influence individual stock prices.

Another problem with fundamental analysis is that you must rely on information provided by the corporation. If a corporation is fudging the numbers or is not entirely truthful, then the future earnings projections will be off.

Another problem is that CEOs give an overly positive slant to the numbers. If a corporation gives out overly optimistic earnings projections, then fundamental analysis will be misleading. You need the skill and knowledge of an accomplished accountant to uncover accounting irregularities.

Still another problem is that you are making assumptions about a company's future prospects that are hard to prove. Furthermore, fundamental analysis doesn't take into account the psychological reasons that drive up stock prices. For example, even though the fundamentals showed that many stocks were overpriced during bull markets, this didn't stop them from going obscenely higher (because of an overwhelming number of buyers).

A final problem with fundamental analysis is that it is extremely time-consuming. Most individual investors don't take the time or have the knowledge to correctly value a company. Professional money managers hire teams of analysts to do fundamental research on individual companies before they invest. Individual investors have to rely on biased research passed down from Wall Street, by word of mouth, or via the Internet. As you know, anything you read on the Internet from anonymous sources is unreliable.

Economic Indicators

Instead of studying individual companies, many professional investors use economic indicators to make forecasts about the overall economy. According to many pros, economic indicators provide insights into where the economy is headed. Economic indicators can also help determine if we're headed into a recession, which countries deserve your investment dollars, and even whether you should buy stocks, bonds, or stay in cash.

When certain economic reports are released to the public, stocks, bonds, and currencies react instantly. Watch what happens when these economic reports (such as the unemployment report) are released at 8:30 a.m. ET. The futures market reacts to the report instantly, and that in turn affects the stock market opening.

Although there are hundreds of economic indicators released on a weekly, monthly, and quarterly basis, only a handful are useful. According to economist and best-selling author Bernard Baumohl, the top three economic indicators are:

1. Institute for Supply Management (ISM) Indexes for Manufacturing and Non-Manufacturing activity.
2. Private-sector employment
3. Personal spending

The monthly ISM report reflects new orders placed to manufacturers, which should lead to more production. The ISM gives an early glimpse into the economy.

In addition, the monthly employment numbers from the Bureau of Labor Statistics are important enough to move the markets in one direction or the other. This report gives some of the freshest data on economic activity and tells us if companies are confident enough about future sales to hire full-time or part-time employees.

Finally, there is the critically important role of personal spending, a statistic that is measured monthly by the U.S. Department of Commerce. If consumers are not actively shopping, the economy is at risk of quickly shutting down. After all, such spending accounts for 70 percent of all economic activity.

Are Americans confident enough about their finances to purchase big-ticket items, such as cars, appliances and flat-screen TVs? If so, this will boost economic activity and possibly light up the stock market. On the other hand, if there are growing doubts about future job security, people will likely curb their spending and save more money, which hampers economic growth and squeezes corporate profits. On the day these economic reports are released, the market can move quite sharply (in anticipation of the results).

Note: If you'd like to learn more about economic indicators, read Bernard Baumohl's book *The Secrets of Economic Indicators* (FT Press, 3rd edition).

Government Reports

There are many other closely watched reports released by the government. For example, the gross domestic product (GDP) is a quarterly report that measures the value of goods and services being produced in our economy. The GDP is very useful and gives a broad barometer of how the economy is doing.

The higher the change in GDP (expressed as a percentage), the faster the economy is growing. If GDP is growing by more than 3 percent, the economy is on the right track. A pace below 3 percent suggests lackluster business activity that could lead to layoffs. And if GDP growth turns negative, the economy has slipped into recession (defined as two or more consecutive quarters of negative GDP).

The government has ways to measure the prices of goods and services and whether they are rising or falling. For example, the consumer price index (CPI) measures changes in prices such as those of housing and clothing. Some people refer to it as the "inflation number" or the "cost-of-living" index. If the CPI goes up, this means that inflation is rising.

The producer price index (PPI) determines whether inflation is rising or falling by measuring changes in the price of commodities that range from raw materials such as steel and aluminum to what it costs wholesalers to produce a finished product. If the prices of raw materials or the finished product rises, consumers will ultimately pay more at the supermarket, department store, and gas station.

. . . .

Now that you have a general idea of fundamental analysis, let's look at another method for analyzing stocks: technical analysis.

Let's Get Technical

If you want to learn about the market, it's essential that you keep an open mind. In other words, become familiar with both fundamental and technical analysis before you buy or sell stocks. Even if you are not interested in short-term trading strategies, it's useful to learn how to use some of the most basic technical tools, which I describe now.

Yes, there are hundreds of mind-numbing tools and charts and patterns, but in my experience, all you need is a handful of indicators. As an investor (or trader), you may not have the time to study technical analysis, but you do need a quick method to confirm whether your stock selections represent a good buy or a big mistake. Technical analysis helps you with those insights.

The ironic thing about technical analysis is that it's sometimes not technical at all. In fact, technical analysis is often easier to understand than fundamental analysis (although not at first).

Have you ever heard the saying that a picture is worth a thousand words? If you have, then you'll appreciate technical analysis because it relies on charts and graphs to help you determine what stocks to buy or sell. In addition, you can use *market indicators* to analyze overall market conditions. The goal is to trade stocks based on indicators rather than on your emotions. In reality, many investors and traders get too emotional no matter what tool they are using.

Note: I wrote an entire book on market indicators, *All About Market Indicators* (McGraw-Hill), aimed at beginning investors. In the book, I included interviews with the creators of the most popular indicators and explained the best way to use each.

What Is Technical Analysis?

By looking at a chart of how stocks have reacted in the past, you can make assumptions about what they might do in the future. This is technical analysis. The shorter the time frame, the more accurate your prediction can be, at least in theory.

As you know, fundamental analysis is the study of the data that affect a company and its long-term business. Technical analysis, on the other hand, is a study of the stock price. It ignores the company and how it conducts its business. Short-term traders primarily use technical analysis to help with buy and sell decisions, although a few traders also use fundamental analysis. In my opinion, it would help the performance of many investors' portfolios if they also checked their stock picks using technical analysis.

Nevertheless, keep in mind that technical indicators and charts are simply tools—there is no guarantee that using them will make you a profitable trader no matter what method you use or how sophisticated your software or equipment. A lot depends on how much effort you put into understanding these stock-picking methods.

The Stock Chart

The key to technical analysis is the stock chart. Although charts are not perfect, in the hands of a skilled technician they do provide important clues as to when people are buying or selling. As I said before, technical analysts believe that looking at a stock chart is similar to a surgeon looking at an EKG before operating on a patient.

You can use charts to help you make statistical assumptions (i.e., predictions) about a stock price or, at the very least, to improve the odds that a trade will be successful.

One of the best reasons for looking at a chart is that it keeps your emotions out of the decision-making process. You may love the company and its CEO, but if the chart shows that the stock is weak and headed lower, you'll probably want to avoid buying it.

The good news is that it's easy to find a stock chart on any company. All financial periodicals and every financial television program—CNBC, Bloomberg, Fox Business News, Yahoo! TV, to name a few—show stock charts. The media discovered a long time ago that one of the easiest ways to show the public how a stock has performed is to display a chart of its price history.

When looking at a chart, the first decision is choosing a time frame. You can select a short time frame—for example, minutes, hours, or a daily chart. Others prefer a longer time frame—a weekly, monthly, or yearly chart (the daily is the most popular). Some traders look at several charts at the same time, each with a different time frame.

Note: The three-month chart is the default time frame on most charting programs.

The Basics

Unless you are planning to trade full time, you'll need to learn only the most important chart patterns. Nevertheless, the following is an introduction to technical analysis and some of the tools and strategies that traders use. Later I show you how to incorporate technical and fundamental analysis into your trading day (or week).

Line, Bar, and Candlestick Charts

There are three main types of stock charts.

Line Charts

A *line chart* basically plots the closing prices of a stock over a specific period. A line connects the price points. Although line charts are easy to read and understand, they are not popular with experienced short-term traders because they don't provide very much information. They are most useful when they are combined with other technical indicators. However, stock analysts on television tend to use line charts because they are so visually appealing. Figure 13.1 is an example of a line chart.

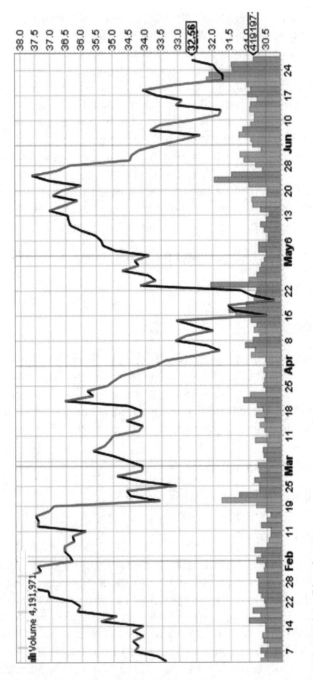

Figure 13.1   Line chart

Source: Chart courtesy of StockCharts.com.

In the figure, you can see that the stock moved as high as $37.50 before reversing. Note the volume bars at the bottom of the chart, which tell you whether there is increased (or decreased) buying and selling. When using technical analysis, it's not important why this stock reversed direction, only that it did, and on higher volume. For example, a stock moving up on higher volume indicates there are more buyers, which is a positive sign for the stock. Conversely, a stock moving down on higher volume is a negative sign. More than likely, it is large institutions such as mutual fund companies or pension funds that are moving the market higher or lower.

Bar Charts

Bar charts are popular with some short-term traders because they are easy to use and understand. The horizontal scale at the bottom of the chart indicates the specific period (in Figure 13.2, three months). The vertical scale displays price. The bar is the range of prices for the period.

For example, the top of the bar represents the daily high, and the bottom represents the daily low. There are also two "ticks" attached to

Figure 13.2 Bar chart

Source: Chart courtesy of StockCharts.com.

the bar, one that extends to the left and one that extends to the right. The left tick stands for the opening price, and the right tick marks the closing price.

You can see at a glance whether the stock closed above or below its opening price. Generally, it is a good sign if a stock closes the day above where it started, especially if there is strong volume right into the close.

Candlestick Charts

Candlestick charts are the oldest form of technical analysis and were created by a shrewd Japanese rice trader who became wealthy using this method. Candlestick charts are popular with many traders because they show so much information, including the psychology of the market at any given time. They are also visually appealing.

Traders believe that understanding the emotions of the market is helpful in determining future trends. Studying candlesticks helps you to see the psychology of the market. One of the goals of using candlesticks is to exit the market before major market reversals. Figure 13.3 is an example of a candlestick chart.

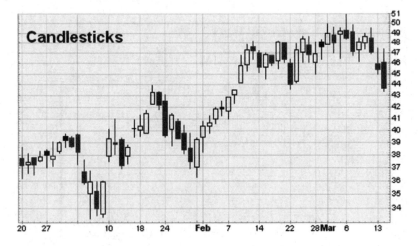

Figure 13.3   Candlestick chart

Source: Chart courtesy of StockCharts.com.

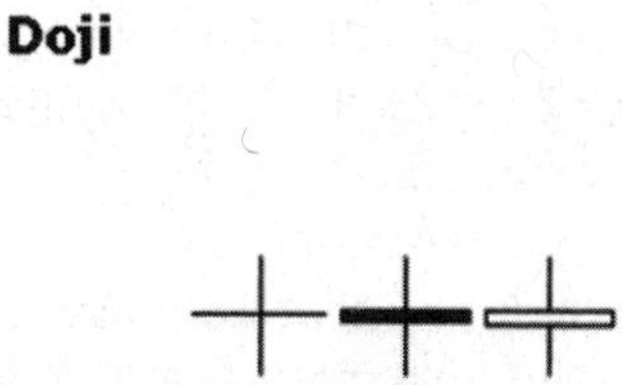

Doji

Figure 13.4   Doji
Source: Chart courtesy of StockCharts.com.

As you can see, the candlestick is made of two components. There is a unique rectangular portion called the "real body." There are lines above and below the real body called "shadows," which indicate the high and low for the day. If you study the shape of the candlestick and the length of its lines, and whether the real body is empty or filled in, you can see who is winning the battle: bulls or bears.

For example, if the bulls are in charge for the day, you will see a tall, white real body. If the bears are in charge, you will see a long, black real body. Also study volume, which helps confirm the move (volume bars are at the bottom of the chart).

There are important patterns that technicians look for. Perhaps the most common is the doji, which shows indecision (see Figure 13.4). It is characterized by small, thin lines and an equal opening and closing price. The cross in the doji is the indecision.

Should you buy or sell based solely on candlestick patterns? No. After recognizing a pattern, confirm the information with traditional technical indicators. Candlesticks are useful tools, but don't buy or sell based only on their signals.

Note: If you are interested in learning more about candlesticks, read the book *Japanese Candlestick Charting Techniques*, by Steve Nison.

Trend Lines

Although I discuss trend lines earlier, let's look at this topic in more depth. One of the main purposes of charting is to spot a trend in its early stages. A trend is simply the direction in which a stock is moving, or is expected to move, over an unspecified time period. Stocks don't move in a straight line, which is why spotting the trend direction is so important.

As you may remember, there are three types of trends: uptrend, downtrend, and sideways. The goal is to participate in uptrends while avoiding downtrends. A saying that technicians use is, "The trend is your friend (until it ends)." The idea is to ride a trend for as long as possible until it runs out of steam. Unfortunately, it's not easy to identify when a trend changes direction.

Let's take a closer look at the three trends.

Downtrend

A stock in a *downtrend* is moving lower and lower. Sometimes stocks move so low that they begin to plunge. If you are holding stock that is in a downtrend, you are probably losing money. Note: Later in this chapter you will learn about *support* levels. When your stock is in a downtrend, but hasn't fallen below support (the price point where buyers previously stepped in to hold up the price), be careful of holding too long. If it does break support, this may be a reason to sell.

Downtrends are frustrating for bullish investors and traders. If you can identify the beginning of a downtrend, it's best to sell or reduce your shares, especially if the stock decline is accompanied by high volume (which means a lot of people are selling). If a stock is in a downtrend and has been for a while, this is also when bottom fishers look for bargains.

A few years ago, people bought stocks when they were in a downtrend because they assumed that the trend was only temporary. This aggressive strategy does work unless a vicious bear market arrives. No matter what you think of technical analysis, it is a mistake to ignore what you see on a stock chart.

Figure 13.5 is a sample screen shot of stock in a downtrend.

Uptrend

A stock that is climbing and has been climbing for a while is in an *uptrend.* For many traders, following an uptrend is the easiest and most profitable strategy. Short-term traders like to buy stocks that are trending higher because they depend on technical analysis for making

Figure 13.5   Downtrend

Source: Chart courtesy of StockCharts.com.

decisions. (Instead of buying low and selling high, traders might buy high and sell higher.)

Just as in a downtrend, traders will look at volume to help determine whether the stock has enough momentum to keep going up. After all, if a stock is moving higher on increasing volume, it is safe to assume that a lot of people, including institutional investors, are buying it.

During a bull market, many stocks are in an uptrend, which can last for months or years. The challenge, of course, is determining how long the uptrend will continue. Sometimes stocks move up so fast that they "break out" above the current price level and move dramatically higher. Sometimes the uptrend ends abruptly. Do not remain bullish forever, but instead follow the trend that you see on the chart.

If the market, or your stock, is in an uptrend, you buy (the "follow the trend" strategy). If the market is in a downtrend, move to cash (or sell short) and wait for the next uptrend. This is easier said than done, but it works remarkably well—that is, if you correctly identify the trend, and if you have the patience to hold during choppy market conditions.

Figure 13.6 is a screen shot of a stock in an uptrend.

Figure 13.6   Uptrend

Source: Chart courtesy of StockCharts.com.

Sideways Pattern

There is nothing more frustrating than watching stocks (or the overall market) go up and down and then end up almost in the place where it began (unless you are a short-term trader). This is called a *sideways pattern*. A sideways pattern is hard to detect, but the stock often stays within a narrow range. It is so random that it's hard to predict which direction a stock is going. Often, the volume in a sideways pattern is very low. A sideways pattern may be a clue that the current trend is ending.

Although it is difficult to trade stocks that are in a sideways pattern, sometimes the sweetest profits come when a stock that is trading sideways for a while (traders will say that the stock is *consolidating*) suddenly breaks violently up or down. The difficult part, however, is figuring out when a new (up or down) trend begins. Because sideways patterns are so challenging, they are more suited to traders than investors.

Note: Being able to evaluate the overall market is one of the keys to your success as an investor or trader. If you can identify the trend, you will have a good idea of when to invest and which stocks or indexes to trade. I am so fascinated by bull, bear, and sideways markets that my latest book is *Predict the Next Bull or Bear Market and Win* (Adams Media).

Trend Reversal

One of the challenges of technical analysis is determining when the current stock trend has run out of steam and may reverse direction. In fact, technicians are constantly on the lookout for the "breaking" of the trend line, which signifies a *trend reversal.* Figure 13.7 illustrates an example of a stock index that has reversed direction.

A short-term trader isn't especially concerned about why the stock reversed direction—only that it did. Identifying this trend reversal and buying into it during the early stages could be very profitable for a

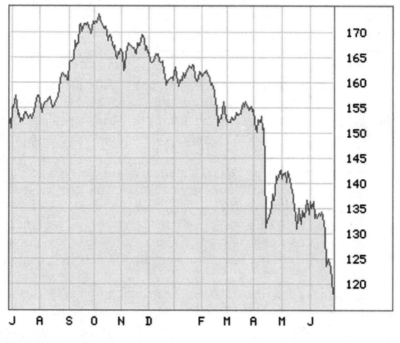

Figure 13.7   Price reversal

Source: Fidelity Investments. © 2002 FMR LLC. All rights reserved. Used by permission.

trader. In this scenario, holding the stock until the trend ends may bring the greatest profits—that is, assuming you can identify the end and sell in time. Experienced traders are constantly looking for other opportunities.

It's extremely difficult to identify a trend reversal before it happens, but sometimes there are clues. For example, a stock in an uptrend may appear to run out of gas, and drop below its *moving averages*, which you'll learn about in Chapter 14. If you do identify a trend reversal, use other technical indicators (in addition to moving averages) to confirm that your analysis is correct and that it is not just a temporary reversal. Also, just because a trend has continued for a long time doesn't mean that it will reverse. Long trend lines are common.

Unfortunately, it's not always obvious that a trend has ended. It takes the courage of your convictions (and the ability to read charts) to exit a winning position. If you truly cannot decide, consider selling half the position. If you see no reason to believe the trend is continuing, then sell the other half. You do not have to get out at the top to make money in the stock market. Do not be greedy. When a trend ends, most people, and especially the media, don't believe it (at first).

For example, if an uptrend ends, most people will still urge you to keep investing (but these people do not understand charts and have no clue the trend has ended), declaring that the bull market is still intact. It takes courage to move to cash when an uptrend has ended or to buy stocks when a downtrend has ended.

On the other hand, and this is important, it's also easy to get out too early. However, you have to base your decisions on technical indicators and charts, and not listen to what "everyone else" says. It also takes courage to stay with the uptrend while everyone else is warning about a market correction or crash. Either way, you have to do what you think is right and not be influenced by the media or opinionated acquaintances.

In addition, don't be stubborn. There will be times when the charts do not give a clear message. During these times, it is acceptable to take the conservative route by hedging, or taking the profits and getting out. I wish that trading stocks were easier, but it's not. On the other hand, many people avoid trading stocks and simply adopt a buy-and-forget philosophy. This strategy works well during bull markets but causes immense pain during bear markets.

Support and Resistance

As mentioned earlier, identifying support and resistance on a chart is extremely important to traders. Let's take a closer look at these two concepts.

When Buyers Win the Battle: Support

Once you learn about support and resistance, you will have a better idea of when to buy or sell a stock. Support and resistance keep appearing on stock charts no matter what method of technical analysis is used. To be a successful investor or trader, however, you will need to understand how to identify support and resistance.

Here's how it works: When a stock is falling, there will be certain prices on the way down where enough buyers step in to buy the shares, thereby "supporting" the price and preventing it from falling further. *Support* is the price level at which a stock price found support the last time it traded down to this level. The theory is that the same price will provide support again. The demand for the stock is thought to be strong enough to prevent the price from dropping further. The buyers are in temporary control.

Support is often at whole dollar numbers because people tend to buy at whole numbers. When looking at a chart, you can often find support levels by studying how the stock reacted in the past. Let's use the three-month chart shown in Figure 13.8 to demonstrate support, which is at $60 per share.

If the stock did drop below $60 per share and continued to fall, technicians say that the stock "broke through support." When this happens, it is not a good sign for the bulls. It means that there aren't enough buyers to support the stock at that price level. When support is broken, it is a significant sell signal.

In the figure, however, the stock did hold support, and did not break through. According to technicians, no matter how good the

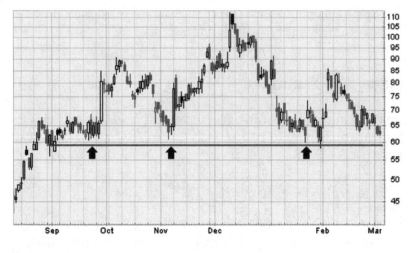

Figure 13.8   Support

Source: Chart courtesy of StockCharts.com.

fundamentals are or how much you love the stock, when the stock breaks through its support level on increasing volume, it's time to sell.

When Sellers Win the Battle: Resistance

When a stock price is rising, there will be certain prices on the way up where sellers step in and prevent the stock from rising further. *Resistance* is the price level at which a stock has stopped rising and sellers take temporary control. When the stock can't go any higher, traders sell their shares, looking for a decline. There isn't enough demand for the stock to cause it to rise any higher. An example of resistance is shown in Figure 13.9.

In this example, the stock tried to break through resistance at $75 per share four times. Once again, sellers prevented the stock from going higher. It then retreated until it reached support at $60.

How do sellers "prevent" the stock from moving higher? They cannot prevent it. However, those who believe that resistance will hold continue to sell the stock. On the other hand, there must be a sufficient number of buyers to accumulate all the stock for sale and continue to bid for more shares, or else the sellers win and resistance holds. However, when the sellers give up or run out of shares to sell, that is when the buyers take charge and the stock moves through resistance.

In Figure 13.9, if the stock had been able to break above $75 per share, technicians would have said that the stock "broke through resistance," and considered that to be a significant buy signal. This indicates that a stock is strong and can be bought as it moves higher. It is common for stocks to break through resistance and go much higher. (By the way, many professional traders wait until a stock breaks through support or resistance before making a trade.)

Warning: Although it is possible to find fantastic stock plays using technical analysis, it isn't easy to master this skill. It is very common for a novice trader to think that technical analysis is easy after making a couple of winning trades.

Here's an example of what could go wrong. For instance, a stock could break through resistance and move much higher. However, after you place your buy order, the stock can suddenly reverse course and

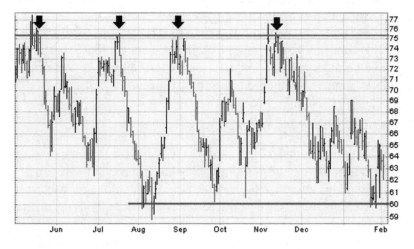

Figure 13.9   Resistance

Source: Chart courtesy of StockCharts.com.

undergo a serious decline. Although technical analysis seems to generate buy signals easily, in the real world some of these signals are false. If every signal were true, everyone would use technical analysis, and there would be no sellers when a buy signal was issued.

Introduction to Stock Patterns

Technical analysts are constantly searching for stock patterns that give them clues to what could happen in the future. One reason the same stock patterns occur again and again is that people tend to make the same mistakes—for example, selling in a panic at the end of a bear market or buying just before a bull market has run out of steam.

It's human nature to follow the crowd, and investors tend to get greedy at the end of a bull market and fearful at the bottom. These emotions show up regularly as patterns on charts. Stock patterns are another tool that technicians use to evaluate what the crowds are doing. In fact, so many patterns have showed up regularly on the charts that technicians began naming them.

Although these chart patterns are not foolproof, they work often enough that technicians make trades based on them. In the hands of a knowledgeable trader, identifying stock patterns may prevent disaster. Unfortunately, being able to recognize stock patterns is difficult. Nevertheless, that shouldn't stop you from trying. With practice, you may be able to identify some basic patterns (see below), but don't invest simply because you see a pattern on a chart. Technicians use other tools to confirm whether the pattern is significant or not.

Head and Shoulders Top Reversal (Bearish)

The head and shoulders is a bearish reversal pattern that shows up often on charts. It indicates that buying has stopped at the top of the uptrend and is about to reverse direction. If you look at the chart in Figure 13.10, you'll see that the pattern really does look like a head and shoulders.

The stock moves higher but pulls back to form the left shoulder. It then moves higher to form the head, which seems bullish. It then falls back to its support level or neckline, which is the alignment of the two support levels.

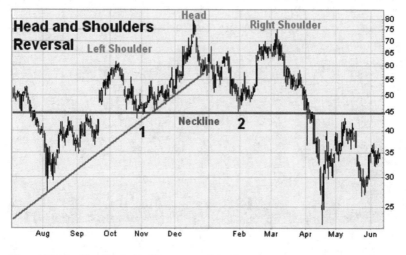

Figure 13.10   Head and shoulders reversal (top)
Source: Chart courtesy of StockCharts.com.

The stock rises again to form the right shoulder but fails to break resistance. Keep your eye on the neckline, because when the stock breaks below the neckline, the chances are good there is profit to be made on the short side (or money can be saved by exiting a long position). The broken neckline confirms that the upward trend of the stock has ended and reversed. In addition, volume decreases as the pattern plays out until it almost disappears. Once the stock falls below the neckline, however, volume may increase if the stock plunges (the result the technician expects to see).

Double Bottom (Bullish—Looks Like a W)

The double bottom is another common bullish reverse pattern. After a downtrend, the stock fails to break through support levels after two attempts and rallies higher, breaking through the "neckline." After the pattern is complete, the trend has changed from bearish to bullish. This may not occur quickly because the stock could consolidate for weeks or months before breaking out to the upside.

Although this is an easily recognizable pattern, the double bottom doesn't always give an actionable signal. Therefore, confirm the pattern with other technical indicators before making a trade. Figure 13.11 is

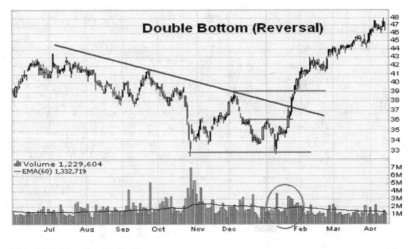

Figure 13.11   Double bottom

Source: Chart courtesy of StockCharts.com.

an example of a double bottom. If the stock fails to break out, it could fall to that baseline once again, forming a triple bottom.

Double Top (Bearish—Looks Like an M)

The double top is another common bearish pattern that shows two peaks at the same price level. After an uptrend, the stock has failed to break resistance after two attempts. If the stock tries to break through the top of the second leg but it fails, and sells off, the double top pattern is complete. The stock could consolidate for weeks or months before the trend changes from bullish to bearish. If the double top pattern is confirmed, it's a clue that you may want to switch from buying to selling. Note the increased volume (circled at bottom of chart) as the trend changes.

Just as with the double bottom, the double top doesn't always give actionable signals. It's easy to spot, but you should confirm the pattern with other technical indicators. Figure 13.12 is an example of a double top.

Gaps

Gaps are simply open spaces in the stock pattern. For whatever reason (perhaps breaking news when the markets are closed), there was

Figure 13.12   Double top

Source: Chart courtesy of StockCharts.com.

no trading at a particular price level, and the stock jumps. Gaps are significant because they indicate strong buying or selling demand. Most gaps occur in the premarket or aftermarket and are clearly visible on a daily chart.

Technicians have identified three types of gaps: continuation, breakaway, and exhaustion. How is this useful? If you own a stock that gapped higher on strong volume, you can continue holding the stock.

If you identify a stock that gaps higher (or lower) but doesn't reach a new high (or low), you might consider selling (it's called an *exhaustion gap*). If anything, a stock that gaps up but doesn't reach a new high might return to *fill the gap* (retreat to the earlier, pre-gap, price).

Advanced note: Breakaway gaps occur when a stock gaps up (moves higher) on higher than normal volume. This may be the start of a significant move, or so the bulls hope. A continuation gap, however, which appears similar to a breakaway gap, occurs about halfway through a trend before pausing, and then resumes trading.

Experienced short-term traders will trade the gap openings, but it's not easy. For example, one strategy is to "fade the gap," that is, trade in the opposite direction of the gap (i.e., selling into the higher gap, or buy the dip on a lower gap opening). This strategy is effective when you correctly anticipate market conditions. If you're a beginner, however, you can learn to identify gaps on a chart, and watch how the stock reacts. Hint: Don't trade gaps until you gain a lot more experience. Figure 13.13 shows an example of a gap.

Problems with Technical Analysis

Critics of technical analysis claim that reading stock charts is similar to telling your fortune using tea leaves. They claim that it's impossible to make predictions about the future based on what happened in the past. Critics claim that there is no proof that technical analysis actually works. (Those who earn their living from technical analysis can only smile at the criticism.)

Just like fundamental analysis, technical analysis is as much an art as a science. It takes a competent and experienced technician to find good stock picks using technical analysis. It takes a lot of time to become competent, so don't expect to learn technical analysis quickly.

One of the problems with technical analysis is that it is extremely difficult to read the signals correctly. If all it took to be successful in the market were sophisticated oscillators and indicators, then most people would use only technical analysis. Although all investors should have a basic understanding of how to read charts and how to use technical indicators like moving averages, this probably won't help for long-term investments (with some exceptions). In general, technical analysis is most useful for short-term trading, while fundamental analysis is more useful for longer-term investments.

Although charting stocks can be profitable, you must also be careful to keep it simple. Otherwise, you may suffer from "analysis paralysis," which means spending so much time studying charts that you don't make trades. Keep it simple—the less complicated the information on your chart, the better.

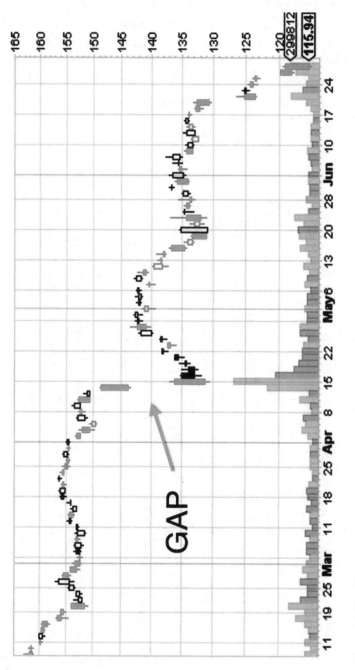

Figure 13.13 Gap

Source: Chart courtesy of StockCharts.com.

167

♦

Bottom line: Many profitable traders rely heavily on chart patterns, including more advanced patterns such as triangles, wedges, and candlesticks, but it takes a long time to learn.

. . . .

In the next chapter, you will learn the tools and tactics that technical analysts use to evaluate stocks.

14

Technical and Sentiment Analysis: Tools and Tactics

Just as with fundamental analysis, there are tools that technical analysts use to determine when to buy or sell a stock. These tools are called *indicators*. All the indicators explained in this chapter can be found on a stock chart (since technicians study stock prices using charts).

By the time you finish this chapter, you should have a better understanding of how to use indicators to provide insights into market (or stock) direction. Just as a carpenter needs a hammer to build a house and a golfer needs the best clubs, traders and investors need indicators.

Using indicators to help with trade decisions keeps emotions out of the trade. When used properly, indicators act as an early warning system, alerting you to potentially profitable or dangerous market conditions. They can also be used to identify when the market or an individual stock might reverse direction. Finally, traders use market indicators to monitor the market trend: up, down, or sideways.

For all these reasons, you should learn about market indicators. Because no one rings a bell when the market has reached a top or bottom, you have to rely on tools such as market indicators to tell you which way the market is blowing.

The main reason you use indicators is to anticipate the market or a stock's direction and put the odds in your favor.

The Market: The Most Powerful Indicator in the World

There is one indicator that is more powerful than any other. That indicator, which is the market itself, always has the final word. That indicator is represented by the major indexes including the Dow Jones Industrial Average, Nasdaq, S&P 500, Russell 2000, or Wilshire 5000, to name the most popular.

Figure 14.1 is a chart of the S&P 500 with a six-month time frame.

Volume: An Underestimated but Important Indicator

Volume shows how many shares of stock are traded over a given period. It is the fuel that drives stock prices higher or lower. By studying volume, you can obtain clues as to whether a stock is moving because of true buying or selling interest or whether other factors influence the price movement. Volume bars appear at the bottom of any chart.

In today's market, billions of shares are traded every day on all the stock exchanges. Most of that volume is generated by institutional traders and high-frequency traders. In fact, one of the ways to follow volume is to determine what institutional investors are doing.

For example, if the market (or your stock) is falling on heavy volume, that is a bad sign. It means a lot of investors (probably institutions) are selling. On the other hand, if the market (or a stock) is rising on heavy volume, it's a clue that institutions such as mutual funds and pension funds are buying.

> *Hint:* If a stock is rising on low volume, it means that the stock doesn't have a lot of institutional support, which is a negative signal.

Sometimes you will hear people on Wall Street talk about a *liquid* stock. This is another way of saying that it is easy to buy and sell shares of the stock. When you buy or sell shares of individual stocks, you want liquidity. For example, a stock without liquidity may be easy to buy, but more difficult to sell at a competitive price.

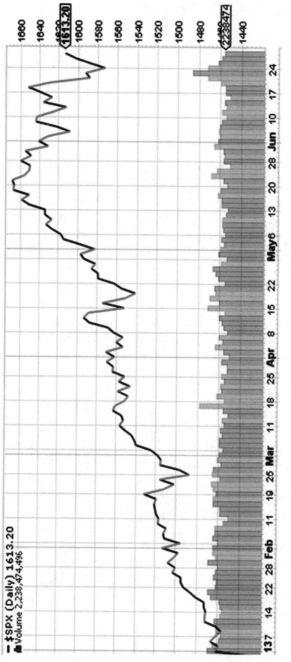

Figure 14.1 Chart of the S&P 500

Source: Chart courtesy of StockCharts.com.

Introducing Technical Indicators

Although there are hundreds of technical indicators, I show you only the ones I consider to be the most useful. You don't need dozens of indicators to make a trade.

Note: Although you will get a good idea of how these indicators work, it still takes time to thoroughly learn how to use these tools.

Moving Averages: Simple but Powerful

One of the simplest but most valuable technical indicators for both investors and traders is the *moving average* (MA). In fact, if I had to choose one indicator to rely on, it would be moving averages. They are easy to use and interpret, and they give valuable clues to market (or stock) direction.

A moving average is the average value of a security's price over a certain time period, such as the last 20, 50, 100, or 200 days. By over-laying the moving average on a chart of the stock or market, you get a visual idea of how the stock (or market) has performed over the speci-fied time period. When plotted on a chart, moving averages appear as curved lines that move higher and lower with each trading day. They offer clues about where a stock is headed.

Many technical analysts use moving averages as *support* (which acts like a floor) and *resistance* (which acts like a ceiling). If the stock price rises above (i.e., breaks through) the moving average, this is seen as a bullish sign. Conversely, if the stock price drops below the mov-ing average, this is seen as bearish and a signal to sell. In particular, many institutional investors use the almighty 200-day MA to define support and resistance. For example, if the stock price moves below the 200-day MA, this is a signal to sell. If the stock price moves above the 200-day MA, this is a signal to buy.

Short-term traders tend to use the 40- or 50-day MA to deter-mine support and resistance levels. It's sometimes uncanny how a stock can nudge up to the 40- or 50-day MA and then immediately reverse direction.

And yet, moving averages are not a silver bullet. Moving averages are slow to react to market conditions, which is why they are called *lagging indicators*. Because they follow prices, they give late signals.

In other words, a stock may have already dropped by 20 percent by the time it finally moves below its 200-day moving average. By then, anyone can see that the stock is in a downtrend. Therefore, it is a good idea to use a shorter-term moving average along with the 200-day MA. After all, the fewer the number of days in the average, the more rapidly the indicator can change.

Although you should not base your trading decisions solely on moving averages (or any other technical indicator), moving averages offer an idea of the strength and direction of the trend.

Figure 14.2 shows a stock chart with two moving averages—the 50-day MA and the 200-day MA.

Note: The squiggly line is the price of the S&P 500 index. The second line is the 50-day moving average. The third line is the 200-day moving average.

MACD (Moving Average Convergence Divergence)

MACD, created by Gerald Appel, appears at the bottom of most stock charts. MACD consists of two lines: (1) a solid black line called the MACD line, and (2) a red line (sometimes dotted), called the 9-day signal line.

Keep your eye on the MACD line. When the MACD line crosses above the 9-day signal line, it is a buy signal. And if the MACD line crosses below the 9-day signal line, it is a sell signal. MACD has had a good record of giving reliable long-term signals.

If you look at Figure 14.3, you will also see a flat line in the middle of the chart called the zero line. (On the chart, MACD is slightly below the zero line, i.e., at −0.393.) When MACD crosses above the zero line, it generates a reliable buy signal. If it crosses below the zero line, that is a sell signal. MACD often fluctuates above and below the zero line. Obviously, you would not buy or sell based only on a MACD signal, but use other indicators to confirm whether the signal is valid.

There is much more to learn about MACD, which I include in my book *All About Market Indicators* (I couldn't resist mentioning it again!). MACD, like any other indicator, is not perfect. Sometimes the signals are not clear, especially at market tops. Also, just as with moving averages, MACD can be a little slow to generate a signal. Still, MACD can keep you on the right side of a trend, which is why it's so valuable.

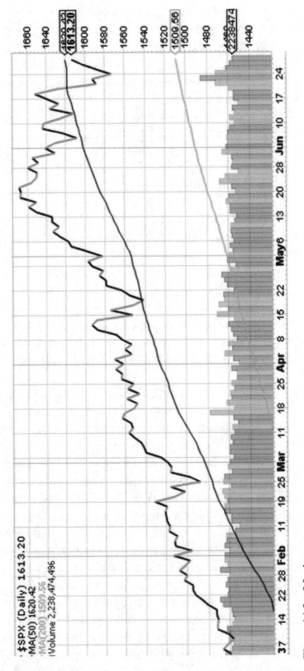

Figure 14.2   Moving averages

Source: Chart courtesy of StockCharts.com.

174

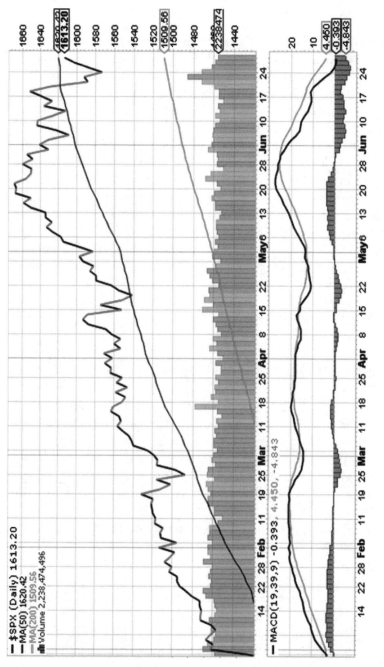

Figure 14.3 MACD

Source: Chart courtesy of StockCharts.com.

175

Other Technical Indicators

If you are new to the stock market, you can begin with moving averages and MACD. Use them to analyze the entire market or individual stocks. If you are fascinated by technical analysis and want to learn more, I've already mentioned my book, but there are other excellent books (look in Chapter 18 for my suggestions). You can also pull up any chart and choose different indicators.

Although there are hundreds of indicators, three other useful technical indicators worth studying are Bollinger Bands, Relative Strength Index (RSI), and stochastics. (These are primarily for experienced traders.)

Bollinger Bands, RSI, and stochastics measure whether stocks are *overbought* or *oversold*. If a stock is overbought, this is a short-term signal to sell. If a stock is oversold, it is a signal to buy. The problem is that stocks can remain overbought or oversold for long time periods before reversing.

It's worth your while to study these indicators closely, especially when using short-term trading strategies.

Introduction to Sentiment Analysis

In addition to technical analysis, you can look for psychological clues that people might be getting too fearful or too greedy. Understanding where the crowds (what Wall Street calls the herd) are investing their money will help you decide how to invest yours. Usually, when you find out where the crowds are investing, it is wise to do the opposite! Sentiment analysis, which I call "reverse psychology," measures the mood of the market.

The following are three useful sentiment indicators.

AAII Survey

One way to measure the mood of the market is by looking at the American Association of Individual Investors (AAII) survey. This weekly survey, which is published on the AAII website and in other financial periodicals, includes the results of a weekly poll. AAII members are asked how they feel about the stock market—bullish, bearish, or neutral.

If more than 60 or 70 percent of the members are bullish, it's a sell signal. If more than 60 or 70 percent of members are bearish, it's a buy. Although people can remain irrationally exuberant for a long time (and also irrationally bearish), these surveys do give important contrarian clues. In the past, the sentiment indicator has been accurate at extreme levels, but the timing has been imprecise. Nevertheless, there are no guarantees this indicator will be accurate in the future.

Investors Intelligence

Another sentiment tool is the Investors Intelligence Advisors Sentiment Survey (II). This weekly survey, published by Chartcraft, polls independent newsletter writers for their views of the market over the next six months.

When more than 60 percent of independent financial newsletter writers are bullish, it's a sell signal. When they are over 60 percent bearish, it's often a good time to buy. Once again, just because sentiment is over 60 percent doesn't mean that you should do the opposite, but you should take notice.

The reason these sentiment surveys work is that human nature never changes. When the market is reaching the stratosphere, many people, even the pros, feel euphoric about the market. Some feel as if they are geniuses for making money in a bull market.

When the market is plunging, people get fearful and gloomy. They tend to avoid the stock market and move their money into cash and bonds. From a psychological viewpoint, when the masses are selling, that is the time to buy, although it's not easy to pull the trigger when everyone else is predicting that the market will go to zero.

The VIX (Chicago Board Options Exchange Volatility Index)

The Chicago Board Options Exchange Volatility Index (VIX) is an index that estimates the future volatility of the U.S. stock market by tracking the *implied volatility* of options on the S&P 500 Index. When you use the VIX as a contrarian indicator, it gives useful insights into what option traders think will happen.

Usually, a spike in the VIX is a signal that a short-term bottom in the market, or an oversold condition, is expected. Therefore, the higher the VIX goes (meaning option buyers are bearish and buying put options for protection), the more likely the market will reverse and move higher.

Conversely, when the VIX declines (because fewer people are buying options in a panic and there is nothing happening to drive prices higher), it is more likely that the market will go lower. The more extreme the VIX reading, the more likely the market will reverse.

It probably seems confusing that if option buyers are bullish, according to the VIX, the market will go lower, and if option buyers are bearish, the market will go higher. However, that is how a contrarian indicator works. Generally, when the VIX goes as high as 40, there is panic in the options world (excess option buying for protection and speculation), so you should consider buying stocks. If it goes over 50, the S&P 500 Index could be near a bottom. On the other hand, when the VIX goes under 20, option traders are relatively calm. If VIX goes below 12, an extreme level of complacency has been reached and traders show no downside fears. The S&P 500 could be near a top when that happens. (There's an old saying: "When the VIX is low, it's time to go. When the VIX is high, it's time to buy.")

Unfortunately, the VIX is not perfect as an indicator. Although it has been effective at identifying emotional extremes, it hasn't been an ideal timing indicator. Although it can tell you a reversal is possible, it can't tell you when.

Bottom line: The VIX has been useful to short-term traders who plot it on a chart with moving averages, but the VIX has not been especially useful to long-term investors. The VIX can remain low for long time periods without generating a significant signal. Nevertheless, the VIX can be used to periodically gauge the mood of the market.

The SEC: Protecting Investors Against Fraud

You may wonder whether there is a government organization that protects the needs and interests of the individual investor. Actually, there is. Congress created the U.S. Securities and Exchange Commission (SEC) in 1934 to regulate the securities industry after the disastrous 1929 stock market crash.

The SEC is something like the police officer for the investment industry. It sets the rules and regulations and standards that Wall Street must follow. The purpose of the SEC (paid for by tax dollars) is to protect individual investors from fraud and to make sure that the markets are run fairly and honestly.

The SEC's website, www.sec.gov, contains helpful articles and resources about the SEC's mission and about individual companies. It's worth mentioning that knowledge is your best weapon against fraud, and the SEC does its best to keep you informed. Unfortunately, not everyone wants a government organization such as the SEC breathing down the necks of corporations and financial institutions. Although Congress created the SEC, there are powerful people with special interests who want to keep the SEC as weak as possible. In fact, some politicians see to it that the SEC doesn't have the funds or resources it needs to go after companies or individuals that break securities laws. (*Note*: Congress controls SEC funding.)

As you can guess, a weak SEC is nothing but an invitation to corporate crooks to use the stock market to finance their illegal trading activities. The low point for a distracted SEC was when Ponzi schemer Bernard Madoff got away with financial fraud for more than 20 years. Unfortunately, it sometimes takes a market crash or the discovery of a huge Ponzi scheme before the SEC is given the proper tools and personnel to go after the crooks.

As an individual investor or trader, you should always be careful about where you put your money. If you do become a victim of a fraudulent investment, it could take years to get your money back, if you ever do. This is why it's essential that you do research before investing. And if you let someone else manage your money, then be even more careful.

Another activity that the SEC monitors is insider trading. There are actually two types of insider trading: legal and illegal. Legal insider trading is that done by company employees (insiders) who file proper paperwork with the SEC before buying and selling shares in their company. These documents are available for viewing on the SEC website.

On the other hand, illegal insider trading occurs when company employees (or their acquaintances) buy and sell stocks based on information that is not known to the public. Do you think insider trading is common? Yes, it occurs a lot more often than many people think. In fact, many insiders still use information they gleaned from their companies to make profitable transactions. Hopefully, a well-funded and strong SEC can go after those who don't want to play by the same rules.

———

In the next chapter, you learn to think outside the box, that is, learn about other investments besides stocks. Feel free to skip the next chapter (which is not an easy read) and go directly to Chapter 16. That is your decision, of course.

PART FIVE

OUTSIDE THE BOX

Options, Bonds, Cash, Real Estate, Currencies, IPOs, and Futures

When most people talk about the stock market, they are referring to buying or selling stocks, mutual funds, or ETFs. There are, however, a number of other investments besides individual stocks. Becoming familiar with other types of investments—for example, *options, bonds, cash, real estate, currencies, IPOs,* and *futures*—will help make you a more knowledgeable investor.

Suggestion: You will find that these alternative investments can get technical at times. Therefore, feel free to skip this chapter for now and continue to Chapter 16. You can always return to this chapter in the future.

Options

You have probably heard about options. Perhaps you have even heard that trading options is too risky. I have a surprise for you. If used properly, options reduce risk when compared to owning stocks. It's true that there are option strategies that are confusing and risky, but let's leave those to the experts. Instead, I introduce you to strategies that can work alongside your stock portfolio.

Note: If you are interested in learning more about options, I wrote a best-selling book for beginners, *Understanding Options, 2e* (McGraw-Hill).

It's true that options can be difficult for some people to understand at first, but it's worth your time to learn a handful of option strategies. In fact, there are four reasons why you'd want to use options:

1. Increase income
2. Protect your stock portfolio
3. Hedge against stock market risk
4. Speculate

These are four of the reasons why experienced traders include option strategies in their portfolios. For example, selling options on stocks you own generates cash flow or income. In a way, you are renting stocks to other people (option buyers), and they pay a premium for that opportunity.

Options are used to protect or insure the value of a stock portfolio. This is a conservative but hardly inexpensive way to use the options market.

Options are also used to hedge risk. For example, if you believe that your stock portfolio may decrease in value (but you do not want to sell your holdings), you can buy put options on an ETF that follows one of the major indexes, such as the S&P 500, Dow Jones Industrial Average, Nasdaq-100, or Russell 2000. If the market goes down, your put will increase in value, offsetting a portion of the losses from your investments.

In addition, options are used as speculative trading vehicles in any market environment (bull, bear, or sideways). Options offer an opportunity to make many times the sum invested (that is known as leverage). The best part of speculating with options is that you know in advance exactly how much you can lose.

Note: If you are new to options, I suggest using options to generate income or to protect your stock portfolio rather than to speculate.

Characteristics of Options

Actually, stock options are contracts that give their owners the right to buy or sell stocks. Every stock option is linked or attached to a specific stock, known as the *underlying stock*. One of the terms used to describe options is "derivative." That means that the value of any option is derived from another financial instrument. Put another way, stock options are derived from stock.

Here's something else you should know about options: 1 option contract represents the "right" to buy 100 shares of stock. Most option buyers eventually sell their options and rarely get involved with a stock position.

Here's the fun part: If you buy a call option, when the underlying stock rallies, so does the call option. If you pick the right stock (known only after the fact), your option will usually return a profit. With leverage, you can make many times your initial investment.

You can also lose money. One of the unique characteristics of options is that they expire after a certain date and time (the *expiration date*). Once expiration arrives, an option is either converted into a stock position or it's worthless.

Because options lose value over time, it is not easy to earn a profit as an option buyer. You have to correctly predict the direction of the underlying stock's movement before the option expires or you could lose your entire investment. Fortunately, it costs much less to buy an option than a stock, but it's still possible to lose it all.

By now, you might wonder why you should consider buying options if it's so hard to make a profit. That's a good question. Instead of buying options, you can also sell the option. If you own at least 100 shares of a stock, you can sell (write) options, and call buyers will pay you cash for them. This strategy is called *selling covered calls* and is considered one of the most conservative option strategies.

Before I explain how to sell covered calls, let's look at two important vocabulary words: *call* and *put*. There are actually only two types of options: calls and puts. With either type of option, you can take only two actions: buy or sell. Although there are dozens of fancy-sounding option strategies, all are based on buying and selling calls and puts.

Call: Buying a call option is similar to "going long" a stock (it means you tend to profit when the underlying stock price rises).

Put: Buying a put option is similar to taking a *short* position in a stock (it means you tend to profit when the underlying stock price declines).

Selling Covered Calls

Now that you have a basic understanding of options, let's take a look at a conservative option strategy: selling covered calls. This is the strategy you use when you own a stock and want to receive income or *premium* in return for limiting upside profits. You can also use this strategy to sell stock that you own. By using the options market to sell stock, you have an opportunity to receive extra cash.

If this is your first time learning about options, don't expect to fully understand all the terms and concepts. But if you can get a general idea of how this strategy works, you can decide if you want to use it one day.

Note: You can begin by selling call options. In return for the cash (premium), you agree to sell shares of your stock at a certain price (called a *strike price*) for a limited time. No matter what happens next, that cash is yours to keep.

Example: In May, you own 100 shares of stock of XYZ Corporation, which is currently $28 per share. Using your brokerage account, find the *option chain* [a list of calls and puts that are available for trading, along with the current market quotes (bid and ask prices)], and select one to sell. Each underlying stock has its own list of options.

You decide to sell one call with a $30 strike price and a June expiration date. This means that the call owner has the right to buy your shares at $30 per share. That right expires when the expiration date arrives (the third Friday of the expiration month, or June in this example). Your only obligation is that you must allow your stock to be sold on the expiration date (for $30, the strike price) no matter how high the current stock price. Even if the stock is $50, you must sell at $30. If the stock is less than $30 (at expiration), then the call owner will elect not to take your shares, and you get to keep them.

When you look at the current bid price for the XYZ June 30 call (the option you plan to sell), it's $2.40 per share. Here's how you can calculate how much money you will receive if you sell one covered call:

$2.40 per share for the June 30 call
× 100 shares of XYZ (equal to one call contract)
Total: $240 premium

Note: If you own 200 shares, then the premium (the cash you receive) for selling two calls is $480.

After selling the call(s), you must maintain ownership of the underlying stock (in this case, XYZ) until the option expires in June. It's a fair trade. In the above example, you were paid a premium ($240) for accepting the obligation to sell those shares at $30.

What could go wrong with this strategy? First, if XYZ declines, you lose money, even after collecting the $2.40 per share. The second problem with selling covered calls is that if the underlying stock (XYZ) goes much higher than $30 per share, you lose out on the gains on anything above $30. No matter how high XYZ goes, you are obligated to sell 100 shares of XYZ at $30 per share. If you think you have a winning stock, selling covered calls limits profits.

The ideal market environment for a call writer is one in which stocks are going sideways or slightly higher. In a sideways market, the stock is unlikely to go very high, which is why writing calls can be a profitable strategy.

Buying Calls

A speculative strategy involves buying call options on stocks. The advantage of buying calls is that you get to participate in a stock that is on its way up without owning the stock. If you are right (which means you are a good stock picker) and the stock zooms higher, you can make many times your initial investment. If you are wrong and the stock does not move higher, or does not move far enough, you will lose no more than your original investment.

For example, if XYZ is $30 per share, it would cost $3,000 to own 100 shares. But if you bought the call option mentioned earlier, it would cost $240 ($2.40 per share × 100 shares). For $240, you are controlling $3,000 in stock.

Example: In May, XYZ is selling for $30 per share. You believe that XYZ will reach as high as $35 per share within the next two months. You look at the market for XYZ call options on the option chain and enter an order to buy one July call option on XYZ with a $35 strike price (expecting the stock to hit $35). The call might cost $2.50, or a total of $250 ($2.50 × 100 shares of stock).

If XYZ reaches $35 or higher on or before July expiration, your call contract will increase in value (for example, it could go from $2.50 to $5.25). The higher XYZ goes, the more valuable the call option becomes. The reason speculators buy call options is that they can profit from a small investment, so there is no need to own the stock.

On the other hand, if XYZ doesn't move beyond $30 per share and you still own it on the July expiration date, you will lose the entire $250.

There are a number of strategies you can use when buying calls. The simplest is to sell the option when satisfied with the profit.

The problem with buying calls is that you must be correct about both the timing and the direction of the price for the underlying stock, or you could lose your entire investment ($250 in this example). If XYZ does not go higher than $30, your option will expire worthless.

You can, however, do well if you buy calls (or puts) right before a major breaking news event. In those situations, expect to pay a high price for your options (because others want to buy them and demand pushes prices higher). Once again, you have to be right about the direction of the move, or the option will expire worthless.

Speculating with options is a difficult way to make money, but there are dozens of other trading strategies, some that are designed to reduce risk.

The next strategy is an example of how you can use options to protect your stock holdings.

Using Put Options to Protect Your Stock Portfolio

Buying protective puts makes sense if you have reason to fear that your stock, or the market, is going to decline, but you still want to hold onto your investments. This strategy helps protect your stock portfolio if a stock gets punished for an earnings miss, or if the whole market declines.

Usually, protective put buyers buy a number of puts (1 put per 100 shares owned) to cover all shares they have in their account. For example, if you own 1,000 shares of IBM and believe that the stock might go down in the short term, you can buy 10 put contracts. If you own 100 shares, you may buy 1 put contract.

Although buying protective puts sounds like a wise idea, you also don't want to throw your money away. If you are so concerned that your stock might plunge, perhaps you should think of selling it rather than paying for protection. Only you can decide if the amount paid for puts is worth the security. Be aware that this protection can be expensive.

Alternative investment: Instead of buying a protective put on an underlying stock, you can hedge your position by buying puts on an ETF such as SPY (S&P 500), QQQ (Nasdaq-100), DIA (Dow Jones Industrial Average), or IWM (Russell 2000).

In my opinion, although those protective puts can be expensive, they help to limit losses in extremely volatile markets.

Bonds

To understand bonds, you have to think like a lender, not an investor. After all, a bond is an IOU. When you buy bonds, you are lending money to the corporation or the government in return for a promise that the money will be paid back in full with interest.

In "bondspeak," the corporation or government promises to pay a fixed rate of interest, let's say 5 percent per year. The amount of interest paid each year (expressed as a percentage) is called a *coupon* (i.e., the interest rate). Basically, this is the amount the bondholder will receive in the form of interest payments. A promise to repay has been made, but that is not a guarantee that either the interest or the principal will ever be paid. That is the risk of bond ownership. At the end of the period (called the *maturity date*), your original money is returned, and you get to keep all the interest.

Wall Street helps corporations raise money not only by issuing stocks, but also by issuing bonds. Technically, a bond is a fixed-income investment issued by a corporation or the government that gives its owner a regular or fixed rate of interest for a specific period.

There are three types of bonds: *Treasuries, munis (municipals),* and *corporate.* Bonds issued by the U.S. government are called Treasuries. They are considered the safest bond investment because they have the full backing of the U.S. government. Munis are issued by state and local governments and are usually tax-free. Corporate bonds have the most risk but provide the highest returns.

There are three categories of bonds: *bills, notes,* and *bonds.* Bills have the shortest maturity dates, from 1 to 12 months; notes have maturity dates ranging from 1 to 10 years; and bonds have maturity dates of 10 years or longer, often as long as 30 years. Usually, the longer the term of the loan, the higher the *yield* will be. (The yield is the annualized return on your investment.)

Bonds may be new to you, so I'll give several examples: Let's say you decide to lend a corporation $5,000 for 10 years. In return, the corporation pays 10 percent a year. This means that for the next 10 years you'll receive $500 each year in interest payments. To review, the bond has a $5,000 face value (how much it will be worth at maturity, and the approximate cost), a 10 percent coupon (a fixed interest rate), and a 10-year maturity (time period). The current market value of bonds is determined by prevailing interest rates and how market participants value the specific bond. That wasn't hard, was it?

Usually, people who don't take a lot of risk buy bonds rather than stocks. With stocks, there is the chance you could lose a good part of your investment. Unfortunately, bonds aren't perfect either. In fact, there are risks in buying bonds.

For example, there is always the chance that the corporation will go bankrupt. This is what happened to Enron, WorldCom, Lehman Brothers, and dozens of other corporations, leaving their bondholders holding an empty bag.

Bonds are given a rating (highly rated AAA bonds are considered the safest). The lower the bond rating, however, the higher the interest rate (because riskier bonds must pay a higher rate of interest to find buyers). Some bonds are so risky that they are called *junk bonds*. For taking extra risk when owning lower-rated bonds, you receive an extremely high yield.

Bondholders are very concerned about interest rates. After all, many bondholders live off the interest payments from their bonds. When interest rates fall, bonds are a desirable investment because the value of the bond increases. When interest rates rise, the value of the bond declines. Generally, bonds are not considered an ideal investment when interest rates are rising.

The inverse relationship between bond prices and interest rates can be confusing. Many people don't realize that bonds trade just like stocks, and the current price varies as interest rates change. The market price of the bond (not to be confused with the bond's face value) rises or falls in the opposite direction from interest rates (inverse relationship).

For example, let's say you purchased a bond for $1,000 with an 8 percent coupon (it pays $80 annually per $1,000 of face value). If interest rates drop below 8 percent, the bond is worth more than $1,000 because investors will pay more to receive the higher interest payments. On the other hand, if interest rates rise, your bond will be worth less than $1,000 because it is less attractive to buyers, who won't pay face value for a bond that pays less than the current interest rate.

To summarize, the advantage of owning bonds is that they promise to pay interest, and also promise that your original money (called *principal*) will be repaid in full. Basically, you lend money and hope the corporation (or other entity) can repay. The disadvantage is that interest rates can rise, severely cutting into the value of your bond portfolio. There is also a small chance that the bond issuer may default and stop paying interest. Nevertheless, bonds are especially popular with people who are more concerned with capital preservation than with making additional money.

If choosing the right bonds seems difficult, don't worry; it is. This is why many people prefer to buy *bond mutual funds*, which allows professionals to make investment decisions for you.

Warning: When buying bonds from a broker or bank, be sure to look carefully at the fees before signing a contract. One of my acquaintances invested $300,000 in bonds with a well-known bank, and when he sold, they charged him a 10 percent sales fee, or $30,000. Don't sign anything unless you read every line, and that goes for bonds, insurance policies, a mortgage, or any other financial endeavor.

Cash

At times, putting your money in cash or a cash equivalent (i.e., *certificate of deposit,* or *CD*) seems like a dumb idea. When returns are no more than 1 or 2 percent per year (or less), the 1 percent return on a CD seems like a bad joke, especially when stocks are rapidly increasing in value.

Sometimes the joke backfires if there is a market correction or crash. During those times, you'd be glad you were holding cash or CDs. That paltry 1 or 2 percent a year will look good compared with the large loss incurred by shareholders.

One percent a year isn't much—in fact, it's a terrible return—but it's better than losing money. (When interest rates rise, however, those low-paying CDs can actually be a wise idea. For example, if interest rates rise and CDs pay 5 percent or more, then this investment makes sense.)

You can also put your money in a *money market fund,* which pays a little more than a bank (which means you will receive very low interest rates). (Basically, a money market fund is a mutual fund that invests in short-term securities such as CDs and *commercial paper.*)

You can also invest directly in U.S. Treasury bills, which offer the advantage of safety because they have the backing of the U.S. government. (Money market funds aren't insured.)

Remember when I talked about diversification? By keeping some of your excess cash in a money market account, you are protected from vicious bear markets. In addition, you can use excess cash to buy your favorite stock or mutual fund when ready. It's also prudent to have extra cash on the side to pay for emergencies and unexpected expenses. There's no rule that says that every cent you have should be invested in the stock market. After all, good financial planning involves having enough cash on hand for emergencies before investing even one penny in the market.

Nevertheless, when CDs are paying less than 5 percent a year, many people accept the low rates because they are afraid of (or don't understand) investing. When interest rates rise, CDs and money market funds will seem like a smart place to park your money (i.e., assets).

Real Estate and Real Estate Investment Trusts (REITs)

One of the smartest investments an individual can make is to buy his or her own home (in my opinion). Not only will you get tax breaks on the mortgage interest but over time your house will likely go up in value. (Of course, there are no guarantees that prices will go up because it depends a lot on your location and the economy. Nevertheless, owning a home is usually cheaper than renting, it allows you to build long-term wealth the old-fashioned way, and, most important, it feels great to be a homeowner.)

The biggest negative of owning a home is that real estate is an illiquid investment (meaning that you can't sell it quickly, as you can when you own a stock or mutual fund). The other downside is that if for some reason you fall behind with your monthly payments, the bank can attempt to take over your home (i.e., foreclose).

Also, when you own a home, you have to pay property taxes, home owner's insurance, and interest on the loan. Even with these drawbacks, owning a home is a worthy financial goal, although it's not for everyone. (For example, renting is simpler and more convenient for some people.)

Many people use real estate as an investment. This includes buying a residential property, such as a single-family home, condominium, or townhouse. You also have the chance to sell it for a higher price or rent it out. As with investing in the stock market, you never want to buy real estate until you have done extensive research.

An alternative to buying real estate is to invest in a REIT, a publicly traded company whose stock can be bought and sold on one of the stock exchanges. These companies purchase and manage various real estate properties.

Note: It is more convenient to buy a REIT mutual fund or REIT ETF.

Unlike real estate, the main advantage of REITs is their liquidity. In addition, REITs offer the benefits of buying and selling real estate without having to do the work. Of course, there is the risk that the company or fund manager will make poor real estate investments, causing the REIT's value to decline. In addition, REITs suffer if interest rates rise because borrowing costs increase. Conversely, REITs do better when interest rates are falling.

Trading Currencies

There are a number of advantages to trading currencies, but many disadvantages. First, the foreign exchange market (forex or FX) is no place for beginners, and it's easy to lose all of your money quickly. Nevertheless, if you're interested, here's a brief introduction to trading currencies such as the euro, yen, or dollar.

The foreign exchange market is very liquid, which means you can quickly get into and out of a trade at any time. Second, forex is open 24 hours a day, five days a week. Another advantage is that forex brokers don't charge commissions; they make their profits off the spreads between the currencies. One of my trader friends quipped, "They make money because you pay too much when buying, and you collect too little when selling."

When you first get started with currencies, you can choose to trade in the currency futures market, which is a physical exchange, or on the forex "spot" market, where you will trade using a broker. If you are a beginner, you'll probably start with the spot market because you don't need a lot of up-front money to get started.

First of all, currencies are traded in pairs, that is, you buy one currency and sell another. For example, if you wanted to sell the euro against the dollar (EUR/USD), a common trade, you could go long the dollar and short the euro (you believe the dollar will go up when compared to the euro). Because there are 28 major currency pairs with eight major currencies, you have a lot of choices.

Another fact: Currencies move up and down by pip (percentage in points), which is 1/100 of 1 percent. One pip equals $10. Although this seems like a small increment, you can theoretically make or lose an infinite amount of money in a day. *The reason:* leverage, which is a benefit and a risk. Because of leverage, with a small amount of money you can make (or lose) a lot more than you initially invested.

It's the high leverage that attracts many traders to the currency market. While the stock market usually gives 2-to-1 leverage, in the currency market, you are allowed 50-to-1 leverage. Put another way, for every $1 invested, you are in control of $50. Therefore, if you plunk down $1,000, you can control as much as $50,000 in currencies. This is the power of leverage, and also how you can lose a fortune.

Unfortunately, many beginners lose not only their initial $1,000 but much more. If you are going to trade currencies, stick with the well-known, large U.S. brokers who are under strict regulatory control.

If you must trade currencies, begin with paper trading. Just as with the stock market, start with small positions and use a strategy. Never forget that you are trading against professional traders who have many more years of experience than you do. Don't expect to make a certain amount each month because there are no guarantees. Wait for the right opportunity rather than constantly trading.

Bottom line: Trading currencies is a difficult way to make money. If you are a beginner, first learn everything you can about the stock market (and then the options market) before even attempting to enter the currency market. Don't forget you can lose your initial investment and much more, which is why trading currencies is not for beginners.

Investing in IPOs (Initial Public Offerings)

Stocks that are being sold to the public for the first time are called *initial public offerings,* or *IPOs.* (Wall Street refers to this process as "going public.") The IPO is an exciting time for the corporation. The biggest advantage for a company when going public is that it allows the company to raise money. It can use this money to expand, pay off debt, or pay for research and development of a new product.

In addition, if the IPO is successful, it can make company insiders extremely rich. There are two types of IPOs: the start-up (a new company that was started from scratch) and the private company that decides to go public.

The company going public hires one or more major Wall Street investment bankers (known as the lead *underwriter*) to manage the IPO process and bring the shares of stock to the secondary market (i.e., a stock exchange), where shares of the stocks will be traded. Current stockholders determine how many shares to sell to the public, and investment bankers help set the initial price range.

Well before any company goes public, insiders (i.e., employees) are often given stock as part of their compensation packages, and now that the company is going public, they can cash in. Meanwhile, investment bankers work with underwriters to create investor interest in the corporation. Underwriters can earn a steep commission for establishing the offering price of the stock, generating interest in the stock, and selling shares to the public through the underwriter's network.

Once the company goes public, research analysts that work for the underwriter may issue buy recommendations on the stock and make positive comments about the corporation. In fact, there is zero chance they will say anything negative, so ignore any buy recommendations.

We saw the power of the IPO when Facebook (Nasdaq: FB) went public back in 2012. The company, valued at over $100 billion, was hyped in the media, which guaranteed a big demand for the shares. In fact, investor demand was so great that Facebook increased the number of shares it planned to sell to the public by 25 percent. Warning: If an IPO is getting hyped in the media, this is a clue that you should not participate, no matter how much you love the company, or its stock. Thousands of retail investors heard about the Facebook IPO and were eager to make a few bucks on a product they knew well. Most observers agreed that this IPO was handled very badly by its lead underwriter, Morgan Stanley (but that was not the fault of the company, Facebook).

On its first day of trading, after a few technical problems, Facebook shares moved a bit higher (10 percent from its offering price), but nothing spectacular. Although the IPO was a success for the company (it raised over $10 billion), investors did not make out as well: The stock slowly fell by 50 percent over the next few months (although a year later, it finally exceeded its IPO price).

As an individual investor without inside connections or access to shares, it is not easy to win the IPO game. Some traders have made small fortunes on IPOs as the shares rallied, primarily because they got in very early (it also helps if you work for a successful startup-that goes public).

If you want to participate in an IPO, however, be sure you read the *prospectus,* a legally binding document filed with the SEC that includes the company's future plans as well as its current financial condition. Even after reading about all the risks, you can always ask your broker for some shares. If you don't get shares at the IPO price, it is advisable to avoid buying. By the time it begins trading on an exchange, it is usually too late to get a competitive price.

> *Hint*: Only the broker's best customers get any shares of the hot stocks at the IPO price.

Futures: Investing in Commodities

The futures market can be traced back to Japan in the Middle Ages, where commodities such as silk and rice were traded in advance of a certain date (although informal trading of futures contracts was recorded in England as early as the thirteenth century). In the U.S., however, the futures market was created in Chicago to help farmers sell their grain in advance of the harvest so they could receive money to lock in the price. Then they didn't have to gamble on the price after harvest.

As a result, in 1848, Midwestern grain traders, along with wealthy Chicago businessmen, created the Chicago Board of Trade (CBOT) as a central location for the buying and selling of agricultural contracts.

In 1865, the Chicago Board of Trade created standardized contracts, called *futures contracts* (or *forward contracts*), for buying grain from Chicago area farmers. The trading of grain and other agricultural products was conducted on the trading floor of the exchange, affectionately called *the pit*. This is the place where members disclosed their bid and ask prices, often by screaming and shouting at each other. This is referred to as *open outcry*. Using hand gestures as well as outcry, they signaled the price and quantity of contracts with the person taking the other side of the trade. Each commodity had its own designated pit.

In 1919, the Chicago Butter and Egg Board, an offshoot of the Chicago Board of Trade, changed its name to the Chicago Mercantile Exchange (CME, or "the Merc"). In 2007, the Merc and Chicago Board of Trade merged to form the CME Group. Although it is guaranteed there will be more mergers and acquisitions, CBOT and CME will be fondly remembered in Chicago as the world's two largest futures exchanges. In recent years, although open outcry is still used for some commodities, the futures exchanges have moved to electronic trading using wireless devices.

The terminology of the futures market is quite similar to that of the options market. For example, a futures contract is a *derivative*, which means its value is derived from an underlying asset such as corn, soybeans, or currency. In fact, the options market is an extension of the futures market and the stock market, based on the successful model created by those exchanges.

In the futures market, people buy and sell commodities such as agricultural items (sugar, corn, coffee), currencies (dollar, euro, yen), precious metals (gold, silver), petroleum products (heating oil, gasoline), interest-rate products (Treasuries), and stock indexes (Nikkei, DAX, Dow).

The futures market is huge and exceeds the number of trades made on the New York Stock Exchange. For example, the equity markets are measured in billions of dollars, but the futures markets are measured in trillions.

When you enter into an agreement in the futures market, you agree to take delivery of the actual commodity. (Imagine what the neighbors will think if 1,000 tons of coffee are dropped on your front lawn.)

The two types of traders who primarily use the futures market are speculators and hedgers. Hedgers use the futures market as an insurance policy or to lock in a price. For example, a company like Starbucks will use the futures market to lock in the price it must pay for coffee and will obviously take delivery.

Speculators, on the other hand, use the futures market to trade. They seek to increase their income by earning trading profits, just as they do in the equity markets. They have no desire to take physical delivery of the commodity. They just want to make money. (Therefore, unless you really want to take delivery of 1,000 tons of coffee, you can simply buy and sell the contracts.)

The futures market uses a form of margining based on the principle of *mark to market*. If a futures contract was worth $1,000 and the contract is worth only $500 by the end of the day, the $500 loss is taken out of your account (in cash). In addition to mark-to-market rules, futures trades are also *cash-secured*, meaning that your account must be paid off or settled in cash by the end of the day. The mark-to-market rule has ruined many unsuspecting futures traders who were forced by the rules to pay for their losses immediately.

· ·

The bottom line is that the futures market, although a useful and necessary trading platform, is not recommended for rookies.

Note: It is useful to look at stock futures before the market opens so you can gauge whether the market will open higher or lower. Go to Bloomberg (www.bloomberg.com) to see the U.S. stock futures or to look at market index prices in other countries.

What Makes Stocks Go Up and Down?

When you invest in the market, you must pay attention to anything that may affect your stocks. Some events seem to come from out of nowhere—perhaps a currency crisis, a war, or an overseas market crash that will wreak havoc on the U.S. stock market. Any one of these events can send the market lower as investors seek protection in cash, gold, or real estate. More than anything, however, markets hate uncertainty.

As an investor or trader, you must be aware of outside events. Sometimes it helps to step back and assess market conditions. If you can anticipate how an upcoming event might affect the stock market, you can shift your money into more suitable investments. In fact, having a thorough understanding of the market environment is as important as picking the right stock. Why? Because in bull markets many stocks go up, and during bear markets even the best stocks can go down.

Why do stocks go up and down? Generally, if there are more buyers than sellers, stock prices rise. If there are more sellers than buyers, stock prices decline. This is Capitalism 101, the heart of our financial system. Nevertheless, at the end of each market day, financial commentators try to explain why the market went up or down, but their explanations often have little to do with reality.

Often stocks rise and fall based primarily on people's perceptions. This is why so many corporations spend a lot of money on promotional advertising and on actions that bring them positive publicity.

Stocks go up or down depending on the mood of the country and the state of the economy. Once again, a lot is based on perception. If people believe that economic conditions are improving and that the country is on the right track, they will be more inclined to invest in the stock market. Conversely, if people are worried about the economy, jobs, or whether we'll go into a recession, they might pull their money out of the stock market.

But this is important: Many times, the stock market goes up even when people are feeling gloomy about their finances, when the economy is struggling, and when the world is in turmoil. This is the power of a bull market, and if we're in one, the stock market will tend to ignore all bad news.

Conversely, if we are in a bear market, the market is likely to react negatively even to good news. Even though the economy might be improving (or will be in a few months), the market continues to go down.

Stocks also go up or down based on the buying and selling of institutions such as mutual funds, banks, and hedge funds. These institutions collectively have the power to move the markets because they trade many shares at one time. In addition, high-frequency traders who trade millions of shares of stock also move the markets each day. With every rumor or important news story, these major market players buy or sell stocks, and this affects market prices.

If there is anything I have learned about the stock market, it's that most people can't predict what will happen next. This is why I rely on market indicators (rather than emotions) to make investing decisions. In addition to using market indicators, I am always on the lookout for clues from other sources.

Following are a few of those outside sources you should monitor.

The Federal Reserve System: A Government Group You Can't Ignore

The Federal Reserve System (the Fed), created in 1913, is so powerful that anything it does influences the stock market. Often, you will hear about the actions of the Board of Governors, a seven-member group that directs the actions of the Federal Reserve System.

The Fed has many duties, including monitoring the economy for problems (especially inflation or deflation) and controlling the country's money supply. It has a powerful tool that directly affects the stock and bond markets—the ability to raise or lower interest rates. The Fed either buys or sells billions of dollars' worth of U.S. Treasury securities, which allows it to adjust interest rates.

Why is this so important? When the Fed lowers interest rates, it becomes cheaper for people to borrow money. After all, many people have to borrow to grow their businesses and buy homes, to name a few examples. After they buy a house, they need furniture, household goods, and appliances. The more money consumers and businesses spend, the better it is for the economy.

Therefore, when interest rates are lowered, the stock market often rallies in anticipation of better times. Conversely, when interest rates are raised, the stock market tends to go down. There's an old saying that is known by most investors, "Don't fight the Fed." When the Fed takes action, it often immediately affects the stock market. Over the longer term, the market is also influenced by the actions of the Fed.

If you are watching the stock market, it is always a big deal if the Fed raises or lowers interest rates. The market may rally on news (or even a rumor) of a rate cut or fall on news of a rise in the rates. Often, the market moves dramatically after a Fed decision.

There is something else you should know about the Fed. Technically, it isn't supposed to care about the stock market, and if you ask the board members, they will say that the market does not influence them. But it's an open secret that they do pay attention. For example, if the market is on the verge of crashing and the economy is teetering, the Fed may intervene with interest rate cuts and by buying massive amounts of longer-term bonds (i.e., what they call quantitative easing).

The bottom line is this: If you are in the stock market, you should pay attention to what the Fed does or says it is going to do. In reality, you can fight against the Fed's moves, but you do so at your peril. Nevertheless, the Fed sometimes makes mistakes, and when it does, the economy pays the price.

The Media

Many people use the media as a contrarian indicator. In other words, by the time something is reported in the media, you might want to do the opposite. For example, when guests appear on television and on the radio gushing about a new economy and an unstoppable bull market, this is a clear warning sign that the markets are overheated and might reverse. It happens all the time, but many people tend to believe what these "experts" have to say.

On the other hand, if you are constantly noticing articles warning of a crash, it wouldn't be surprising if the stock market is about to take off higher. Why? Because most financial columnists and TV hosts have a terrible record of predicting what the market will do next. One of the reasons you are reading this book is to help you analyze the market on your own so you don't have to listen to opinionated but wrong-headed authorities, including many that appear on TV. When you gain experience, you'll learn that the market has a mind all its own, and doesn't care what anyone else thinks. The market is the "Great Humiliator," as one money manager said.

Nevertheless, the media are very helpful in warning of possible trouble. The key is figuring out what is important. Sometimes seemingly irrelevant news buried in the back pages of the newspaper or the Internet is the most important.

The Dollar: I'm Falling and I Can't Get Up

One economic indicator that you should keep your eye on is the dollar. When the dollar is strong against other currencies, such as the yen and euro, foreign investors will buy our Treasuries and invest in our stock market. That's the good news. The bad news is that the strong dollar makes our goods undesirable to foreigners (and exports decline) because they are expensive. A strong dollar also makes it hard for people to travel to the United States because it is so expensive.

On the other hand, when the dollar is falling and is weak against other currencies, foreigners may pull their money out of our stock market. (Basically, they get hit twice, once when their U.S. stocks fall in price, and again when they lose money on the currency.)

If the dollar is falling, it is not a good time to travel overseas because it is more expensive. Perhaps the only positive thing that comes from a weak dollar is that foreigners can afford to buy our goods and services, which pleases U.S. manufacturers (as exports rise).

Bottom line: If you are in the markets, keep your eye on the strength or weakness of the dollar compared with other currencies.

Inflation

Inflation refers to the rate (as a percentage) at which the prices of the goods and services increase each year. When studying economics, you learn a lot about inflation. One of the reasons that people invest in the stock market is to try to beat inflation, that is, to increase their net worth by more than the effects of inflation.

For example, suppose inflation is currently at 1 percent. This means that it costs 1 percent more to buy goods and services than it cost one year earlier. When you go shopping, you find that the prices of groceries, cars, and homes are higher. Because of inflation, the McDonald's hamburger that cost you 15 cents in 1959 now costs $1.20. A seat at the movies that cost 25 cents back in 1960 now costs $10.00. That is the power of inflation.

Note: Many people forget that although the prices of goods rise over time, wages also rise. When hamburgers were 25 cents, the minimum wage was $1.00 an hour. And although a movie ticket might now cost $10, moviegoers earn a lot more now than they did in 1960.

Inflation that is too high is not good for the economy, which is why the markets respond negatively. It means that people are getting less for their dollars. Conversely, low inflation is good for consumers because they can afford to borrow, charge purchases on credit cards, and buy houses. The more consumers spend, the better it is for the economy.

One of the reasons that investing in the stock market is a good idea is that historically the market has handily beaten inflation, returning an average of 11 percent. Of course, there is no guarantee that the stock market will come close to returning 11 percent this year or next or over the next 20 years (in fact, during bear markets, market declines can be excessive).

Note: Each month, the Bureau of Labor Statistics (BLS) prints inflation rates along with other fascinating data such as the unemployment rate, average hourly earnings, consumer price index (CPI), and labor productivity.

Deflation: An Unusual Nightmare

To understand deflation, let's review what we mean by inflation. When the price of goods rises each year, when everything costs more, this is inflation. Deflation, on the other hand, is an economic condition in which prices of goods and services fall. Although inflation is common, deflation is quite rare in the United States (Japan, however, was in a deflationary environment for over two decades).

To the uninformed, deflation seems like a good thing. The prices of nearly everything fall as the supply of goods piles up. Manufacturers are forced to cut prices to entice buyers. On the other hand, companies cut employees, real estate prices fall, and the stock market goes through a rough period. Prices are low, but few people have the money to buy anything. Those who do have money tend to wait for prices to drop even further.

One of the best ways to protect against deflation is to get out of debt. That means paying off credit cards, car loans, and possibly the mortgage (although you should talk to a tax advisor before doing the last of these).

In addition, force yourself to save more. If we really do have a deflationary environment, those with the most cash will prosper. Because deflation is so unusual in the United States, there is no need to be especially concerned. Just keep a close eye on economic conditions and be prepared to act if economists alert you to a deflationary environment. (To be honest, even many economists can't agree what economic environment we're in.) In my opinion, however, getting out of debt and saving money is a good idea no matter what the economy is doing.

Booms and Bubbles

A *bubble* is a phenomenon in which investors and traders pursue stocks (or other items) at such a feverish pace that prices rise to irrational levels. Buyers seem to be under a mass delusion that the market can only go higher. Before long, speculators hoping for quick profits jump in, creating a mania. Eventually, investors come back to their senses, buyers disappear, and prices fall. That can lead to a selling panic. There have been a handful of bubbles in history, all of which ended quite badly for investors.

One of the most spectacular bubbles in history occurred in Holland in the seventeenth century. In 1635, people were willing to pay nearly any amount of money to own a single tulip bulb. These bulbs became status symbols for the rich and famous, including the Dutch royals. Some of the bulbs were beautiful mutations, what the Dutch called "bizarres." Speculators would buy one and then immediately sell it for a higher price.

As the tulip mania increased, speculators pushed prices higher. For example, to buy one exotic tulip bulb, you would have to exchange several horses, pigs, bread, a carriage, cheese, beer, and house furnishings (using today's exchange rate, well over $200,000).

The entire country got swept up in the mania. As with most bubbles, most people didn't know they were in one until it was too late. At the time, people thought that the tulips were wise investments that would last forever. Many investors were more than willing to trade their houses or valuable paintings for one tulip bulb.

In addition, some speculators, to juice their returns, bought and sold options on the tulip bulbs. As the (call) option prices climbed, speculators would sell them for even higher prices. Some people made fortunes without ever taking possession of the tulips. Also, some tulip dealers bought put options (called "time bargains") as a hedge in case the tulip prices dropped.

In 1638, the bubble popped rather abruptly and dramatically. Suddenly, the extreme tulip prices plunged. People looked around and wondered how anyone could have paid so much for an exotic flower.

It was similar to a game of musical chairs when the music stops. People who only a few months before hadn't been able to buy the tulip bulbs fast enough now couldn't sell them in time. Family fortunes were wiped out, there was widespread panic, and the Dutch economy collapsed.

The 1929 Stock Market Crash

The U.S. also has had its own share of bubbles. When the 1920s began, the stock market was generally for the idle rich who bought and sold stocks at their leisure. Stock prices were volatile and moved up and down through most of the decade. By 1927, however, there was a strong upward trend (i.e., a bull market) and even small investors became enamored of the stock market.

With the introduction of buying on credit, members of the middle class were able to buy autos, washing machines, vacuum cleaners, clothing, and radios—items that previously only the wealthy could afford. At the same time, steel production and manufacturing increased.

As a result, the stock market boomed, a fact that was constantly publicized in the newspapers. "It's a bull market!" the headlines blared. Soon, everyone dreamed of getting rich by investing in stocks, including people who had never invested before. Some people thought the stock market would rise forever.

Those who couldn't afford to buy stocks could buy on margin with very favorable interest rates. Margin requirements were as low as 10-to-1, so if you had $1,000 to invest (a small fortune in those days), the brokerage firm would lend you an additional $9,000.

It seemed as if everyone was in the stock market. As more and more people entered the market, the prices of stocks went higher and higher. In a way, it was like a huge Ponzi scheme.

The attitude of the Coolidge administration was laissez-faire, a French term meaning "let things be." The U.S. government wanted to let the forces of capitalism work without interference. As the stock market got shakier and the economy got worse, the new president, Herbert Hoover, realized that something had to be done. The goal was to tighten margin requirements without causing panic. Unfortunately, investors panicked.

After a series of frightening stops and starts, the market finally crashed on October 24, 1929. Over $10 billion of investors' money was wiped out before noon. Huge crowds of angry and shocked investors packed the visitor's gallery of the NYSE to watch the debacle. By noon the market was in a "death spiral."

Investors around the world were horrified at the extent of the financial damage. By October 29, 1929, all the market's gains from the past year had been wiped out (but that was just for starters). Over the next three years, the market fell 89 percent from its 1929 high of 381.

One of the reasons the market crashed in 1929 was because of margin. As the stock market fell, people who had bought stocks on margin didn't have the money to pay back what they owed. That's when investors had to sell stock at any price just to raise cash to repay their margin debt. Banks and brokerages stepped in to take possession of people's savings accounts, houses, and anything else they could get. The market went from a boom in 1928 to a bust in 1929.

After the crash, economists tried to figure out what had gone wrong. It was obvious that many people had missed the signs that the market was overpriced. For example, the P/Es of many stocks were extremely high, well beyond the P/E historical norm of 15. In addition, the Federal Reserve (Fed) decided to raise interest rates, which many economists considered to be the wrong move. Congress also had a hand in turning a recession into a full-blown depression. For example, during this period, it doubled income taxes and raised tariffs on imports and exports.

Another problem was that banks were allowed to operate with few restrictions on how much they could lend. After the crash, many of the banks' customers had no way of paying back the money they had borrowed, forcing many banks to close. Finally, many people believed that fraud and insider activity was to blame. After the initial crash, the United States entered a three-year bear market. The Dow finally bottomed at 41 in 1932.

The new president, Franklin Delano Roosevelt (FDR), took a number of unprecedented steps to bring stability and trust to the market. In 1934, the president created the Securities and Exchange Commission (SEC), the government agency charged with making sure that the stock market is run fairly and protects investors.

Wall Street was skeptical about letting the government interfere with the private sector, but the steps the government took eventually helped turn around the economy. However, it took 25 years for the Dow to make it back to 381. Most people who bought in 1929 never lived to see their stocks get back to even.

Although the market has had its share of booms and busts over the years, the 1929 crash and depression was an extremely rare event, one that we hope isn't repeated in the future.

The Internet Bubble
In the late 1990s, many Internet stocks surged by dozens of points a day, turning many people into paper millionaires. Investors were deluded into thinking that all Internet companies would make a fortune, and their stocks would continue to go higher.

Companies such as Excite@Home, Pets.com, HomeGrocer. com, and hundreds of others were bid up to ridiculously high prices. At the time, some Internet companies with no earnings had a higher market cap than some of the largest corporations in the United States.

The Internet bubble ended badly. Many of the smaller Internet companies went bankrupt, but even the stocks of well-known technology companies plunged. People who were once millionaires were now holding nothing but worthless stock certificates. Although the Internet was one of the most influential discoveries in history, if you were holding the wrong Internet stock, you could have lost everything.

Less than 10 years later (at the beginning of the twenty-first century), there was also a housing bubble, which resulted in the doubling and tripling of housing prices. Some people made fortunes buying and selling houses without ever taking possession of the houses (i.e., flipping). The entire country was swept up in the housing mania, and no one imagined that housing or stock prices could go down. Ironically, the housing bubble also helped fuel another stock market bubble (along with low interest rates).

Just like the tulip bubble, the housing and stock market bubble ended abruptly. Investors looked around and wondered how they could have paid so much for stocks with little or no earnings, and many houses that were bid up suddenly plunged, creating a foreclosure crisis.

The housing crisis also helped to crash the stock market. Those who were holding stocks saw the value of their portfolios fall by 50 percent or more. Even stocks in some well-known financial companies fell by as much as 80 or 90 percent. Big-name companies like Lehman Brothers and Bear Stearns declared bankruptcy.

Although housing prices remained low for years afterward, the stock market did bounce back after a few years. Unfortunately, many investors were so afraid of another market crash that they avoided the stock market altogether, missing out on one of the strongest bull markets in U.S. history. Booms and bubbles: that is often the story of the stock market.

In Part Six, you will enter the opinion section of the book, where I tie all the loose ends together and offer advice and suggestions. You are free to ignore my opinions if you wish, but you should find the last section quite interesting.

SINCERE ADVICE

Why Investors Lose Money

I've learned a lot from interviewing some of the top investors and traders in the country, as well as from my own mistakes and successes in the stock market. One of the reasons this chapter is valuable is that I help you avoid the errors I've made in the market (and I've made quite a few).

As you will learn from experience, the mechanics of the stock market are relatively easy. The hard part is making money, and one reason investors don't make money is because of mistakes.

There is nothing wrong with making mistakes. Actually, the biggest mistake of all is not recognizing that you made one. Fortunately, I studied my blunders and worked hard not to repeat them.

There is something else you should know: Many investors listen to the wrong people, get too emotional about the market, buy and sell based on fear and hope rather than on facts, and don't have a set of rules.

My goal in writing this book is to help you not be like everyone else and to outline the tools and strategies you need to succeed. These are not secrets, but are based on trial and error. Most of the time, our worst enemy is ourselves.

The Most Common Mistakes

The following are the most common mistakes that investors make. As you gain experience in the stock market, there will be certain mistakes you'll make more than once. The goal is to avoid repeating any mistakes, but especially the ones that cause the most trouble.

Mistake 1: Not Selling Losing Stocks

Failure to get out of losing positions early is probably the number one reason why so many stock accounts are destroyed. For a variety of reasons, primarily psychological, people hold onto their losing stocks far too long.

 If you sell a stock for a loss, you may deride yourself for not having sold sooner. Adding insult to injury, you have to admit that you lost money. No matter the sale price, it always seems as though you could have done better. It's true—you can always do better. But that's in the past, so you shouldn't beat yourself up. It's the next trade or investment you should think about. Also, it's not a mistake to lose money, because not every trade can be a winner. But it is a mistake to let a small loss turn into a much bigger one.

 One reason small losses get bigger is that some people think that they can't be wrong about their stock picks. Others convince themselves that the stock will come back one day. (It might, but meanwhile you missed out on dozens of other stocks that are already on the move.)

 At the beginning of a bear market, many people do not get out when their stocks fall by 10 or 15 percent, and sometimes they buy more shares (buy-on-the-dip strategy). Although there was still plenty of time to exit the market with relatively small losses, many people hold or add to their losing position.

 It often takes months of a bear market before people realize that they have held too long. (By the time you've lost 80 or 90 percent of your investment, perhaps it really might be too late to sell unless you want a tax write-off.)

 As I've said earlier, if you lose more than 7 or 8 percent on an investment, sell. (If I lose more than 5 percent, my 5 percent rule, this is a warning sign. I then put the stock on my alert list. If it does not recover and continues to fall, I will sell it without hesitation.)

You lost money, and your expectations weren't fulfilled. Game over, so sell the stock. The main point is to take action when your stock is losing money. If the company looks fundamentally strong, if the stock is going down and breaking below support (for reasons that may not be immediately apparent), there is only one response: Sell.

Note: Occasionally there are exceptions. If you buy a stock at what appears to be the bottom and it makes a long sideways move before losing 7 or 8 percent, it might be acceptable to hold it, especially if technically strong (i.e., has not broken support).

Other exceptions: If a stock goes down in a bull market, it is possible to buy on the dip and still make money. To be successful when buying on the dip, you must really know the stock well and study how it behaves.

For example, if a strong stock constantly moves between $40 and $45, the next time it goes to $40, you could buy. Short-term traders would sell near $45 per share. Long-term investors can consider holding longer, but verify by looking at the chart and confirming with technical indicators.

> *Hint:* If you follow this one rule, you will save yourself a small fortune over time. Do not argue with the market or the stock. If you are losing money on a stock (or any other asset), sell before the losses become too painful. Holding onto losing positions is not recommended.

Mistake 2: Allowing Profitable Trades to Turn into Losers

There is nothing worse for the ego (and your portfolio) than watching a profitable stock turn into a loser. Sometimes it's less painful to have never made money in the market than to have won and lost it. Some people who fall in love with their stocks have a difficult time believing that their favorites won't return to even (or back to their highs).

As you gain experience in the market, you will hopefully invest in strong stocks in leading companies. In my opinion, however, if a stock starts pulling back from its high, or hits your sell target price, sell.

Note: If you are a brilliant investor like Warren Buffett or Peter Lynch and you know how to calculate the true worth of a company, perhaps you can hold certain stocks indefinitely. But for us mortal investors who don't have the resources to hold for decades, selling to lock in gains (and especially to cut losses) makes sense, at least to me.

If you are holding a winning stock position and making money, it can also make sense to add to the position. In other words, add to winning positions and sell losing positions. It sounds simple, but it's very hard for people to do. Even if you don't want to add to a winning position, don't make the mistake of selling a winner too early.

Bottom line: It's not easy to manage winning stock positions. On one hand, you don't want to sell too early and miss out on future gains. On the other hand, you don't want to sell too late and lose all of your profits.

Mistake 3: Getting Too Emotional (About Stocks)

One of the main reasons that people lose money is they get too emotional about their stocks. It's not surprising. After all, when real money is at stake, it's easy to fall in love with your stocks when winning and be too afraid to act when losing.

Sometimes you have to do the opposite of how you're feeling. In fact, sometimes the right decision is the one that seems to be the most uncomfortable. After a correction or crash, it's not easy to buy. More than likely, you may feel like avoiding the stock market altogether. You must not succumb to fear and panicky decisions by putting all your money in a savings account at the market bottom.

Conversely, when the market is reaching all-time highs and investors are giddy about how much money they're making, it's difficult to resist the crowd. When others are feeling overconfident, perhaps thinking they are geniuses in a bull market, you must remain unemotional.

Reduce your stock positions, hedge your holdings, or reallocate assets. It's easy to forget that in bull markets the positive sentiment can change quickly. Be on the lookout for signs of a market slowdown or reversal.

To refresh your memory, some of the signs of a potential market reversal include: the market is going higher on declining volume, leading stocks are faltering, there is a strong market opening but a weak close, and there is more than a day or two of weak closes. All these clues indicate that institutional investors, who collectively move the market, are selling.

Long after you have read this book, there will be other bull and bear markets. If the market is falling by 10 or 20 percent, remember to stay calm and look for an opportunity to calmly reenter the market. There is no need to go all in to try to seek the bottom. This is not the time to listen to panicked acquaintances who will "never invest in the stock market again" or who predict the end of the world as we know it.

It's also dangerous to your wealth to be influenced by other people who are too emotional. I've lost too much money listening to opinionated investors and traders who were convinced they were right, and seemed knowledgeable. They'd yell and scream and write angry e-mails about how the market "shouldn't go up!" But it does (or vice versa).

One of my acquaintances told me a half-dozen reasons why the market shouldn't go up (government debt, inflation, problems in other countries, etc.), but the market was bullish despite his warnings. Everything he said was a legitimate concern, but he missed out on one of the greatest bull markets in history.

Almost as harmful to your portfolio as fear and greed is hope. In the award-winning movie *The Shawshank Redemption,* the movie character Red (played by Morgan Freeman) said, "Hope is a dangerous thing." In love as in life, there is always hope that things will work out in the end. In the stock market, however, hope can wreck your portfolio. If the only reason you are holding onto a stock is because of hope (and not for fundamental or technical reasons), you will probably lose money. Typically, investors are hopeful when they should be afraid, and afraid when they should be hopeful.

The best attitude you can have is a neutral one. Don't come into the market with preconceived ideas of how much money you are going to make (always a bad sign) or that the market is going to go up or down. Let the market be your guide.

Using technical or fundamental indicators for guidance, having a strategy, and sticking to that strategy are a lot more useful than coming up with an opinion and waiting for the market to agree with you. Don't forget: Only the market is right. Everything else is just noise.

Mistake 4: Not Having a Plan for Buying and Selling

I've mentioned this earlier, but it's worth repeating. If you don't have a plan, then you're flying blind, perhaps relying on tips or impulses to make investing decisions. For example, you might wake up one morning and decide to buy gold simply because you read a positive article about that idea. Or you might decide to sell one of your profitable stocks on a whim because of something you heard on television.

The main point is that you should have a plan. If you don't, you are vulnerable to making impulsive decisions and listening to wrong opinions, dumb tips, and bad advice. Have a plan and stick to it unless something in the market or in the company changes.

Mistake 5: You Are Not Disciplined and Flexible

Most people lose money in the market because they are not disciplined. If you are disciplined, you have a strategy, a plan, and a set of rules, and no matter what you are feeling, you stick to your strategy, plan, and rules. Discipline means having the knowledge to know what to do (the easy part) and the willpower and courage to actually do it (the hard part). This has always worked for successful investors and professional traders.

Although discipline is essential, you also need to balance this with a healthy dose of flexibility. Some investors are so rigidly disciplined about sticking with their stock strategy that they stop thinking and blindly follow their plan. Markets do unexpected things and you must react when the market and stocks turn against you.

In the name of discipline, some rigid investors refuse to admit defeat. Discipline is essential, but you must be realistic enough to realize that your plan could be a losing plan. You have to be flexible enough to change your plan, and your rules, under unusual conditions. Nevertheless, it is not the time to suddenly show flexibility when you are losing money. That is the time to cut those losses before they grow too large. For every rule and strategy, there are exceptions. It takes a really exceptional investor to be both disciplined and flexible. If uncertain, stick with being disciplined. Being flexible means having an intelligent alternative.

Mistake 6: Trading on Tips

If your eyes glaze over when you read about fundamental or technical analysis, there is a simpler way to find stocks to buy—stock tips. The beauty of tips is that you can make money without doing any work. If this sounds too good to be true, it is.

In fact, one of the easiest ways to lose money in the market is by listening to tips, especially if they come from opinionated blowhards on financial programs, well-meaning acquaintances, or columnists. These people often become cheerleaders for a stock, trying to convince you to buy (and sometimes sell). Because it's hard to say no to what seems like easy money (especially when the tip comes from a trusted source), there are some steps you can take to limit your risk.

First, you should never act on a tip before doing your own fundamental or technical research. You can also find stocks by using a stock screener (your broker will have one). Most people spend more time researching a new television than a stock. Many people wouldn't think twice about spending $10,000 on a stock tip but will spend a month researching a $600 television set.

If you do receive a "can't lose" tip that is impossible to resist, buy in small quantities. If the tip turns out to be a dud (and it probably will), you've lost only a little money, and you've also learned a valuable lesson.

Note: If you receive a tip, another relatively inexpensive idea is to buy one or two call option contracts. With a call option, you know in advance how much you can lose if the stock doesn't go up. Buying a call option, although a speculative strategy, will cost less than buying stock.

Should you get your stock picks from experts? Often, experts who appear on television or are quoted in magazines are terrible stock pickers. Nearly anyone connected to the financial markets is optimistic about the market. If the market goes down, the experts tell you to buy because the price is so low. If the market goes up, they tell you to buy because if you don't buy now, you will miss out. I'd be very cautious about buying or selling stocks based on what you hear on television, radio, or the Internet.

Mistake 7: Trading During the First 15 Minutes of the Trading Day

Are there really times of the day when it's difficult to trade? Based on my observations, the most volatile time to place a trade is the first 15 minutes of the trading day. (That's also why you shouldn't place orders in the after-hours market. It's not always volatile, but on some days it is.)

During the market open, automated market orders and panic trades are being processed. As the market attempts to find its way during this volatile period, some technical indicators give false signals (especially lagging indicators).

Also, in the last 15 minutes, many traders close their positions. Because this period can be so volatile and indecisive, novice traders may want to avoid it.

Note: As you gain experience, this time period can also be lucrative because volume is often high and it's easy to get filled.

Mistake 8: Holding Losers and Selling Winners

Most people hold their losing stocks, hoping they'll come back to even. They also sell winning stocks early to lock in profits. Unfortunately, strong stocks that are moving higher often keep moving higher, and stocks that are losing value often keep falling.

There are many exceptions, but generally, if you hold onto your winning stock positions and get rid of losers, you should see a huge improvement in your investment results. Most people do the opposite: When they have a winning stock, they sell as soon as they have a small profit, sometimes missing out on the biggest move. And when they have losing stocks, many tend to hold, hoping they will get back to even.

One strategy investors use is buying on the dip, where investors buy more shares of a favorite stock as it drops in value. Although at times this strategy may work, in my opinion, this is a risky strategy. More often than not, the stock keeps falling. I've seen this happen with many leading stocks, especially technology and financial stocks that seemed invincible. In a down market, any stock can plunge. Another lesson: Stocks can go lower, or higher, than you ever thought possible.

Mistake 9: Not Using Market Indicators

No matter whether you're an investor or a trader, you should look at market indicators. As you learned in Chapter 14, there are dozens of indicators. The most powerful, of course, is the market itself. You should get in the habit of watching the overall market for clues.

For example, if the market is going higher, is it rising on strong volume or weak volume? Is the market starting off strong in the morning and ending weak in the afternoon? That is bearish. Or is it starting weak in the morning and ending strong at the close? That is bullish.

In addition, use basic indicators such as moving averages to determine the direction of the trend. If the trend is up and it's a bull market, use bullish strategies. If the trend is down and it's a correction or a bear market, use bearish strategies.

Mistake 10: Not Keeping Track of Mistakes

One of the advantages of being a beginner investor is that it is not surprising if you lose money. I know that sounds harsh, but it's the tuition that almost every investor pays when he or she is first starting out. The key, however, is to keep your losses to a minimum by trading only small dollar amounts and by not borrowing money to invest.

Making mistakes is expected, but you should not repeat the same mistakes over and over. We all have our vulnerable spots. Some people buy stocks based on questionable tips, others hold their losers too long, and others invest without having a solid strategy. When you make mistakes and lose money, write those mistakes in a trade journal.

In your journal, list the reasons why you bought a stock, where the idea came from, and what you expect from the stock. Also list the date, the cost, and commission. Write your target price, the price at which you plan to cut losses, and your planned exit price. If possible, describe the technical pattern that encouraged the trade decision. Your goal at first is not to make a fortune (although that would be nice) but to be a better investor. If you can do that, instead of investing or trading for a few weeks or months, you can learn to trade for a lifetime.

Mistake 11: Not Planning for the Worst

Before you get into the market, be prepared, not scared. Although you should always know that profits are possible, be prepared for the worst. The biggest mistake investors make is thinking that their stocks won't go down. They are not prepared for an extended bear market, a recession, a correction, or an unanticipated event that damages their portfolio. Even if you don't expect a financial disaster, know when you will cut losses and exit. Base your plan on logic and common sense, not fear.

One of the reasons I survived even after making many mistakes is that I use a number of strategies that protect my portfolio, especially if I see evidence that the current trend will end. When I am certain (based on indicators), I sell when the uptrend is struggling, or I buy when the downtrend has reversed.

Based on technical or fundamental analysis, if you believe a correction or bear market is imminent, here are a few steps you can take to protect your portfolio:

1. *Sell stocks and move into cash.* Cash is a comfortable place to be when the economy is struggling and the market is falling. Temporarily waiting on the sidelines in cash until the market recovers is a comfortable choice. If the market really does capitulate, one way to win is to be flush with cash when stocks are selling at bargain-basement prices. When you are in cash (including Treasury bills if the economy gets really terrifying), it's easy to make unemotional decisions about where to put your money next.

The problem with cash, as you know, is that you could lose money to inflation. But that is better than losing more money in a bear market. Still, having money on the side for emergencies is a helpful antidote to fear.

2. *Study more.* If we do enter into a lengthy bear market, use the time to study the markets, read books, and focus on learning fundamental and technical analysis. When the market does come back (so far, it always has), you'll be prepared with a handful of new stock ideas.

Conversely, if we are in an extended bull market (and you are not in cash), I find it helpful to read books on the crash of 1929, or the book *Manias, Panics, and Crashes* by Charles P. Kindleberger. This will help keep you grounded and on the lookout for signs that people are irrationally exuberant. I also enjoy reading about the struggles of short seller Jesse Livermore in the book *Reminiscences of a Stock Operator* by Edwin Lefevre.

3. *Have bear market strategies:* Although selling short is not recommended for beginners, you can buy inverse nonleveraged ETFs that earn money when the market declines. Use them as a hedge against long stock positions or as a stand-alone play to profit in a down market. You can also buy put options for protection when the market goes down.

Important: Corrections and bear markets do not typically last longer than a year (of course, there could be exceptions), so don't hold short positions for too long. Have an exit plan, just as you do when going long.

Mistake 12: Believing the Market Is Logical

Unfortunately, the market and its participants are not always logical. As British economist John Maynard Keynes once said, "Markets can remain irrational longer than you can remain solvent." If you are looking for logic, play chess. The market often acts irrationally, which is why so many very intelligent, logical people lose money in the market. The economy could be struggling with high unemployment and high government debt, and the market could still go much higher.

Bottom line: The only reality is what the market does, and everything else is just noise.

Mistake 13: You Don't Know How to Lose Money

This may be hard to believe, but the best way to become a better investor is to lose money. Most experienced investors and traders believe that you learn more from your losers than from your winners. In fact, one of the worst things that can happen is that you think it's easy to beat the market (especially in a bull market). Before you have a chance to cash in your winnings, most of your profits may disappear.

If you lose money in the stock market (or in any other financial endeavor), turn this event into an educational experience. Believe me, I speak from experience. I learn much more from my losing stocks than from my winners. Determine whether the strategies you (or your financial advisor) are using are on the right track. To protect yourself against mistakes, learn how to limit your losses and protect your winnings.

As I have said repeatedly, losing money is expected, but refusing to cut losses shows a lack of discipline. One of your goals is learning how to handle losing positions (as well as winners). That means having the discipline to have a trade plan, cutting losses, and having the patience to wait before taking on a position.

Take Action

As I said before, if you lose more than 7 or 8 percent on a position, it's not the time to make excuses and pretend they are only paper losses. Remember that in the market, everything doesn't work out as expected. Those 8 percent losses can easily turn into 50 percent disasters. That's why it's essential to cut losses at some specified level.

Next, closely review your investment strategy. You should analyze each of the stocks you are still holding. If you are losing money (the only scorecard that counts), you might want to sell the losers now and reevaluate.

. . . .

And now, in the next chapter, you will learn where to get help if you want to learn more about the stock market.

Where to Get Help

If you are a novice investor (at least you were before you read this book), you may want to do additional research, including looking at websites and books devoted to the stock market.

I start by giving you a list of the books I think will be helpful.

Books

For Rookie Investors

How to Make Money in Stocks (McGraw-Hill, 2009) by William J. O'Neil. How to profit in the market with a rule-based, systematic approach.

One Up on Wall Street (Simon & Schuster, 2000) by Peter Lynch and John Rothchild. How to profit in the market using a long-term investment approach that includes observing what people are buying at the mall or other stores, and knowing the companies before you buy their stock.

The Little Book of Common Sense Investing (Wiley, 2007) by John Bogle. A short book on the advantages of using index mutual funds and why they should be in every investor's portfolio.

Neatest Little Guide to Stock Market Investing (Plume, 2013) by Jason Kelly. An introduction to the stock market that is similar to my book but includes Kelly's investment strategies.

For Rookie Traders

Reminiscences of a Stock Operator (Wiley Investment Classics, 2006) by Edwin Lefevre. A must-read classic about the trading experiences of Jesse Livermore, a legendary trader from the early twentieth century.

A Beginner's Guide to Short-Term Trading (Adams Media, 2008) by Toni Turner. An easy-to-read book for novice short-term traders that includes trading tactics and tools.

Trading for a Living (Wiley, 1993) by Alexander Elder. How to master the psychological challenges of the market as well as how to use technical indicators.

Market Wizards 2nd Edition (Wiley, 2012) and *The New Market Wizards* (Harper Business, 1994) by Jack Schwager. The author delves into the minds of profitable traders in these two classic books.

How I Made $2,000,000 in the Stock Market (Martino Fine Books, 2011 reprint) by Nicolas Darvas. Old but relevant classic of how a stock market novice makes a fortune in the stock market using support and resistance and pyramiding.

For Experienced Investors

The Intelligent Investor Revised Edition (Collins Business, 2006) by Benjamin Graham. A classic book aimed at value investors on how to use fundamental analysis to determine whether a company (and its stock) is a good buy. Graham also discusses the reasons that investors are unsuccessful.

The Secrets of Economic Indicators 3rd Edition (FT Press, 2012) by Bernard Baumohl. This is an extremely readable book on understanding and interpreting economic indicators. After reading this book, you will know a lot more about economics than you thought possible.

Useful Websites for Investors and Traders

*Paid subscription required.

Finance.yahoo.com (Yahoo! Finance)
Money.cnn.com (Money)
www.aaii.com (AAII)*
www.barrons.com (Barron's)*
www.bigcharts.com (BigCharts)
www.bloomberg.com (Bloomberg)
www.briefing.com (Briefing)
www.candlecharts.com (Candlecharts)
www.cnbc.com (CNBC)
www.fool.com (Motley Fool)
www.foxbusiness.com (Fox Business News)
www.forbes.com (*Forbes* Magazine)
www.ft.com (*Financial Times*)*
www.google.com/finance (Google Finance)
www.investopedia.com (Investopedia)
www.investors.com (*Investor's Business Daily*)*
www.kiplinger.com (Kiplinger)
www.marketwatch.com (MarketWatch)
www.money.msn.com (MSN Money)
www.moneyshow.com (MoneyShow)
www.morningstar.com (Morningstar)
www.nasdaq.com (Nasdaq)
www.nyse.com (New York Stock Exchange)
www.sec.gov (SEC)
www.seekingalpha.com (Seeking Alpha)
www.sigfig.com (SigFig)
www.stockcharts.com (Stockcharts)
www.thestreet.com (The Street)*
www.tradersexpo.com (Trader's Expo)

www.valueline.com (Value Line)*
www.wsj.com (*Wall Street Journal*)*

. . . .

Now that you have read about where to get help, I'll tell you about
some of the lessons that I learned in the market.

Lessons I Learned from the Stock Market

Fortunately, I am free to tell you what I really think about the stock market. You don't have to agree with what I say. In fact, I welcome opposing viewpoints. There is no one right answer when it comes to the stock market. In the end, you will have to make up your own mind about where and how to invest your money.

It's the Sitting and Waiting That Makes You Money

I learned the following from Jesse Livermore: Once you set up a long-term stock position, give it time to develop into a winning position as long as it doesn't violate your selling rules. Some of my worst mistakes were selling a winning position too soon, before I was able to make big money. (As you know, I also believe in limiting losses. Livermore didn't at first, which is why he went bankrupt three times.)

One time I spent two weeks setting up a long (bullish) position in anticipation of a positive Fed announcement. I bought one or two stocks and index funds that I thought would benefit from the announcement (it was rumored that the Fed would keep interest rates low).

A week before the announcement, my stocks moved higher, and I had a decent profit. Fifteen minutes before the Fed announcement,

I received a call from a professional trader friend of mine. He said, "The market is going to crash!" And then he hung up. It was a chilling tip, one that I should have ignored.

Instead, I got scared. I didn't want to lose my meager profits, so I sold all my long positions. After all, my friend (who worked for a major bond firm) knew more about the Fed than I did. At 2:00 p.m. that afternoon, the Fed made its announcement: It decided to keep interest rates low. The market reacted by moving higher by more than 250 points that day and another 100 points the next day.

I learned a few lessons that day. First, I won't allow myself to be influenced by other investors, even those who know more than I do. I also learned to stick with my strategies, and not change my mind too quickly. Even though I made no money on that trade, what I learned helped me save a fortune in the future.

Use Both Technical and Fundamental Analysis

Nearly every book written on the stock market assumes that you will choose between technical and fundamental analysis when deciding which stocks to buy. Guess what? You can use both methods. If you're an investor, you can learn a lot by looking at a stock chart, using technical indicators, and looking at basic stock patterns. At the same time, unless you are making a short-term trade, you should not buy a stock unless you are convinced that the company's fundamentals, especially earnings, are strong.

Although there are advantages and disadvantages to both methods, by using fundamental and technical analysis, you can study both the company and its stock price. Not only will you become a more knowledgeable investor or trader, but you will also have more tools. This could give you an edge over other market participants. Rather than choosing one method or the other, use both.

Buy and Protect

In my opinion, you shouldn't simply buy a stock and hold it indefinitely, that is, buy and hold. Unfortunately, many people buy and forget, hoping they'll make infinite profits over the long term. For years, investors have been lured into using this simple but questionable strategy. Let's try to understand why buy and hold is so popular.

First, there has been a massive public relations campaign by Wall Street to convince investors to buy and hold stocks. If the market is going up, you buy because you could miss out on the next bull market. If the market is going down, you buy because stock prices are cheap. In reality, history has been on the side of this strategy. Historically, the S&P 500 has returned an average annual return of 11 percent, but there are no guarantees that this will continue in the future.

When the public invests in the market, it keeps people on Wall Street employed. This is why most pros advise clients to buy stocks. Hardly anyone advises selling. Sell a stock? Are you kidding? It will always come back one day, they say. During corrections, people are buying and hoping that their portfolios will miraculously come back to even by the time they retire. Many will be in for a huge disappointment.

Many advocates of buy and hold point to the successful record of billionaire investor Warren Buffett. The experts don't tell you that Buffett almost never buys technology companies, and that he has the skill to take apart and analyze a balance sheet and the patience to stick it out for the long haul.

Unfortunately, it's not easy for people to emulate Buffett. Most investors don't take the time (or have the skills) to do the necessary research, they get too emotional about their stock picks, and they often buy the wrong stocks. In addition, blindly holding individual stocks during a bear market is dangerous to your wealth.

Instead of buy and hold, buy and protect. Your goal is to make money in bull markets while attempting to limit losses in bear markets. After all, there is nothing more damaging to your portfolio and your ego than watching helplessly as a bear market viciously destroys 50 percent or more of your portfolio. You can buy and hold while the market is going up, but protect your portfolio before the bear market does real damage.

The Markets Are Not Fair to Individual Investors

If you are going to participate in the stock market, you must know the truth: The markets are not fair to individual investors. If you look behind the scenes on Wall Street, you will find manipulation, lies, distortions, and other schemes that allow company insiders and Wall Street players to maneuver around the rules. The individual investor, unfortunately, is usually left in the dark.

Other offenders are penny stock manipulators. These include companies with questionable accounting practices and pump-and-dump schemes.

In my opinion, the biggest game of all is trying to convince people that the markets are fair and equitable and that everyone has an equal chance to make money. The truth is they are somewhat fair, but it's not a level playing field. The insiders get information faster than retail investors, and have the high-speed equipment to buy and sell in microseconds. For example, if a major market-moving event occurs overnight, before the U.S. markets even open, Wall Street already has a head start (being able to trade overseas the instant that the news event occurs), leaving individual investors to play catch-up.

Of course, it doesn't have to be this way. It will take a combination of government intervention (including a stronger and well-financed Securities and Exchange Commission), politicians who are willing to stand up to Wall Street's special interests, and investors who are unwilling to participate in an unfair game. Until the market is truly fair, individual investors would be advised to be careful.

Risks and Rewards

Every good book has a surprise ending, and I will not let you down. Here is mine: After participating in the stock market for most of my life, I've concluded that most people, especially beginners, should not buy or sell individual stocks. Surprised? Although I believe that people should learn everything they can about the market, overall I think that most investors should buy and sell index funds. I know this is an unusual conclusion from someone who wrote a book about stocks. (And believe me, I know this is not a popular position to take!)

In my opinion, buying and selling individual stocks is an extremely tough game to master. I think that some individual investors don't have the time, the knowledge, or the discipline to make good stock-buying decisions. You can't just buy a stock and go to sleep. You have to monitor individual positions, and, unfortunately, most people don't have the discipline or time to do that. They just buy and hold, which can be a losing strategy with most individual stocks, especially when the portfolio is not carefully monitored.

I do believe that you can occasionally speculate with individual stocks (with a small portion of your portfolio), and perhaps invest in stocks when a good opportunity arises, but most investors cannot beat the market on a regular basis. In fact, most professional investors can't beat the market.

Therefore, if you buy index ETFs, instead of beating the market, you will make money by following the market. In bull markets, you can do very well. If a bear market approaches, and you can get out early, then either reduce your position or stay away from the market completely and move to cash until the market stabilizes.

Note: If you don't have the discipline or confidence to get out of the market at the right time, and then get back in at an appropriate time, then you'd be better off buying and holding an index fund through the good times and bad. If you are a retail investor, however, I still don't recommend buying and holding individual stocks (and never during a sideways or bear market).

How to Make Money in the Stock Market

If you are excited by the stock market and feel that you can make money at it, by all means, set aside a small sum of money and begin. It is not surprising to make 10 to 20 percent on one stock. Stocks such as Google and Apple went up by much more than that over time, and there are many more examples.

Even if you don't have much money right now (you will one day), lessons learned about the stock market are priceless. As long as you are aware of the risks (that you could lose money), go ahead and start investing (but start small).

Right now, you might be feeling a little overwhelmed by all the information I included in this book. Remember this: The easiest part of investing is buying. The hard part is making and keeping a profit. One mistake that many beginners make is entering the market without a clear idea of what to buy. They just go out and buy any stock they heard about, perhaps from someone on TV or a neighbor. This is a huge mistake.

Before you put real money in the market, it's important that you create a strategy for buying and selling stocks. In this book, I introduce a number of investing and trading strategies. If this is the first time you've learned about the market, you probably want to know which strategy is best.

The answer: It depends! It depends on how much risk you are willing to take, your time horizon, and what type of securities (stocks, mutual funds, index funds, or ETFs) you want to buy.

Nevertheless, if you are a beginner, below are three strategies that can help get you started. These strategies are not "get-rich-quick" schemes but are designed to help you build wealth over time.

Here are the three strategies that work if you have less than $3,000 (or more if you have it). If you are a beginner, your first goal is to learn everything you can about the stock market (which is why you're reading this book).

Strategy 1 :Invest in a 401(k) or an IRA.

Think of the stock market as one part of a larger financial plan. At first, you will get a job or start a business in order to build up enough cash for emergencies and investing. If you work at a company, it probably has a 401(k) plan or stock purchase plan. In my opinion, these are fantastic ways to build wealth. Just be careful about putting all of your assets into the company that employs you.

Often, you can purchase stocks (or index funds) at favorable prices. Many of the plans are tax-deferred, and often the employer will match contributions. First, talk to a tax professional or the plan administrator for the exact rules.

Speaking from experience, it is amazing how you can build wealth over the long term in a tax-deferred plan with matching contributions. There are no guarantees that you will make a profit, but with the help of the advice offered in this book, you will be on the right track.

Strategy 2: Buy an index fund.

Buying index funds (or no-load mutual funds if you want to pay more for an active manager) is an excellent way of learning how the stock market operates. You can buy index funds through your brokerage firm or as part of your company 401(k) or IRA. If you've never invested before, stick with big name fund families. Start your research at Morningstar to get ideas of which funds to buy. Remember, although last year's performance is no guarantee of future performance, start with index funds and ETFs that have low management fees and good long-term records (longer than five years).

Index ETFs or index funds that follow the major market indexes are an inexpensive way to enter the stock market. As you may remember, more than 80 percent of active managers do not beat the indexes each year. Put the odds of earning money in your favor by simply investing in the index and saving money on management fees.

As you gain experience, you can also buy ETFs that follow sectors or industries that you know well. Although ETFs provide instant diversification, you can diversify further with stock, bond, international, and commodity ETFs.

Strategy 3: After you gain experience with index funds and ETFs, you can buy individual stocks.

Although many people don't have the time to study which stocks to buy, opportunities do arise. Now that you've read my book, you know how to invest in the market. You can start by buying a few shares of one or two leading stocks that have good prospects for the future. Then apply the strategies learned in this book to manage your holdings and earn a profit.

If you are a trader, you can attempt to buy low—or buy high and sell higher on momentum. As long as you are investing small sums, you can try several appropriate trading strategies included in this book.

Buyer Beware

Before you enter the stock market, you should know that you are entering a battlefield populated by sharks who want your money. If you are going to invest in the market, you must fight them with knowledge (an effective shark repellent).

If you aren't willing to do your homework (independently do research on stocks or use market indicators) and must depend on a stockbroker or a stranger on television to tell you what stocks to buy or sell, you are destined to lose money.

Remember that investing money in the stock market is serious business. In the end, you must take responsibility for your own investment decisions. Sometimes investors and traders made money in the market but have no clue as to how they were doing it. "I'm doing nothing, and look how much money I'm making," several investors told me. You should not be surprised to learn that many of these people eventually lost most of it (when the bull market ended).

. . . .

Congratulations for finishing my book! Before you go, I have a few closing comments.

The Closing: What You Should Do Now

Now that you are aware of the risks as well as the rewards of the stock market, you have a choice. If you are willing to take the time to learn what works for you and your financial goals, you can survive and prosper as a twenty-first-century investor. Fortunately, you have more tools and information than any investor had in the past. As soon as you put down this book, begin thinking and planning. Don't stop until you have created a successful trading plan, strategy and investment portfolio. My advice is to keep it simple and to start small. Always be on the lookout for profitable money-making opportunities while remaining cautious.

Another goal is to build up enough confidence so that you can invest or trade independently. If you have the confidence to manage your own account, you will be able to invest for a lifetime and not be forced to depend on others for advice. (It's very liberating, but challenging, to manage your own account.)

Finally, I have learned from experience that the best investment you can make is in people. You can't go wrong spending money on an education, a home, a new business, your children, or those who desperately need your help. After all, why make money if you don't use it to improve your life or the lives of others?

It's been a pleasure sharing my knowledge and experiences with you, and I wish that all your financial dreams come true. Before I go, I'd like to share with you a letter written by my grandfather, Charles Sincere, a successful owner of a Chicago stock brokerage firm (a *Wall Street Journal* article with similar advice was attached to the letter).

The letter contained the following financial advice to his son (my father):

1. Begin by paying off all your debts.
2. After being debt-free, you must not be tempted to blow your money on risky financial ventures.
3. It is hard enough for most people to earn a bare living, including 95 percent who are unable to keep and acquire a fortune. This is not to discourage you but to warn you and give you courage to fight harder to be one of the 5 percent.
4. Always be prepared for the possibility that you may have to support your parents.
5. You want the privilege of helping those who are afflicted and impoverished.
6. The most important measure of success is integrity, hard work, and being right more than 55 percent of the time. This also means diversifying risks so that when you are wrong, it won't break or crimp you.
7. Never cosign promissory notes to help others.
8. Never buy stocks in small corporations to please friends—easy to buy, hard to sell.
9. Don't be easy in loaning money except in extreme cases (i.e., don't let a worthy friend down).
10. Only hard experience, proven by facts, should impress you and cause you to follow the rules just outlined.

Index

Note: Italic page locators refer to figures and tables.

Brokerage firm(s), 5
  choosing a, 37–41
  full-service, 39–40
  money managers, 40–41
  online, 37–38
Bubbles, 207–208, 210–211
Bucket shops, 117
Buffett, Warren, 9–10, 33, 77, 114,
  131, 218
Bull markets, 16–17, 92, 109,
  158, 217
Bureau of Labor Statistics (BLS),
  144, 206
Buttonwood Agreement, 6
"Buy and protect," 234–235
"Buy" recommendations, 138
Buy-and-hold strategy, 76–78
Buying calls, 187–188
Buying strategies (*see* Investment
  strategy[-ies])
Buy-on-the-dip strategy, 78, 217

C

Calls, 186
  buying calls, 187–188
  selling covered calls,
   186–187
CAN SLIM system, 101–104,
  107–109
Canada, 7
Candlestick charts, *152,*
  152–153
Capital gains, 5
Capital losses, 5
Cash, 105, 192–193, 224
Cash accounts, 41–42
Cash-secured trades, 199

CBOT (Chicago Board of Trade),
  197–198
CEOs, 128–129, 143
Certificates of deposit (CDs),
  192–193
Charles Schwab, 38
Chicago Board of Trade (CBOT),
  197–198
Chicago Board Options Exchange
  Volatility Index (VIX), 177–178
Chicago Mercantile Exchange
  (CME), 198
China, 7
CME (Chicago Mercantile
  Exchange), 198
CME Group, 198
Coca-Cola, 8, 26
Commercial paper, 192
Commissions, 6, 14, 38, 39, 77
Commodities, 197–199
Common Sense on Mutual Funds
  (Bogle), 109
Common stock, 5
Compound interest (compounding),
  31–32
Compounded earnings, 32
Congress, 179
Consumer price index (CPI), 145
Coolidge, Calvin, 208
Corporate bonds, 190
Corporate insiders, 129
Corporations, 5, 8–9
Cost-of-living index, 145
Coupons, 190
CPI (consumer price index), 145
Currencies, 194–195
Custodians, 41

Acknowledgments

To Zach Gajewski and Peter McCurdy, my editors at McGraw Hill, for working with me to develop this book and helping me to see it through to completion.

I want to thank Mark Wolfinger for fact-checking the entire book, and for making exceptional suggestions and corrections.

I want to thank William O'Neil and John Bogle for taking the time to discuss market strategies with me.

I also want to thank Hazel Garcia, for always being an excellent assistant; Paula Florez, for helping to transcribe tapes; Kathleen Sherman and Amy Smith from *Investor's Business Daily* (IBD); web designer Ryan Saunders, for creating top-notch websites; Jonathan Burton of MarketWatch.com, for the writing opportunities; and Laura Libretti at McGraw Hill, for her wise advice about the publishing world.

I also want to thank my friends: Lourdes Fernandez-Vidal, Alexandra and Angela Bengtsson, Harvey Small, Sanne Mueller, Karina Royer, Luigi Silvestri, Lucie Stejskalova, Jarle Wirgenes, Lene Wirgenes, Jason Zimmer, Rayna Exelbierd, Evrice Cornelius, Maytee Martinez, and Maria Andersson.

About the Author

Michael Sincere interviewed some of the top traders and financial experts in the country to find out the lessons they had learned in the market so that he could help others avoid the mistakes he had made. He wrote a book about these lessons, followed by four more books, including *Understanding Options* (McGraw-Hill, 2nd edition), *All About Market Indicators* (McGraw-Hill), *Start Day Trading Now* (Adams Media), and *Predict the Next Bull and Bear Market and Win* (Adams Media).

Sincere has written numerous columns and magazine articles on investing and trading. He has also been interviewed on dozens of national radio programs and has appeared on financial news programs such as CNBC and ABC's *World News Now* to talk about his books. In addition to being a freelance writer and author, Sincere writes a column for MarketWatch, "Michael Sincere's Long-Term Trader."

You can visit the author's website and blog at www.michaelsincere .com. Using indicators and personal observations, each week he writes about the market's next move.